THE TIBETAN BOOK
OF THE DEAD

THE
TIBETAN BOOK
OF THE DEAD

*The Great Liberation
through Hearing in the Bardo*

by GURU RINPOCHE
according to KARMA-LINGPA

Translated with commentary by
FRANCESCA FREMANTLE
& CHÖGYAM TRUNGPA

SHAMBHALA
Boston & London
1992

Shambhala Publications, Inc.
Horticultural Hall
300 Massachusetts Avenue
Boston, Massachusetts 02115

9   8   7   6   5   4   3   2

Printed in Singapore on acid-free paper ⊗
Distributed in the United States by Random House, Inc.,
and in Canada by Random House of Canada Ltd

Cover art: Mandala of Samantabhadra, Supreme Buddha,
© Musées Nationaux (Musée Guimet, Paris).

See page 257 for Library of Congress
Cataloging-in-Publication Data.

ISBN 0-87773-675-8
LC 91-50798

CONTENTS

EDITOR'S NOTE

This Shambhala Pocket Classics edition of *The Tibetan Book of the Dead* is a reprinting of the Shambhala Dragon Edition of the same title and includes the complete translation of the *Bardo Thötröl,* the original introduction by Francesca Fremantle, the full commentary by Chögyam Trungpa, the "Inspirational Prayers," and notes. The pronunciation key, glossary, bibliography, and index have been omitted.

FOREWORD

The *Bardo Thötröl* (*Bar-do'i-thos-grol*) is one of a series of instructions on six types of liberation: liberation through hearing, liberation through wearing, liberation through seeing, liberation through remembering, liberation through tasting, and liberation through touching. They were composed by Padmasaṃbhava and written down by his wife, Yeshe Tsogyal, along with the sādhana of the two mandalas of forty-two peaceful and fifty-eight wrathful deities.

Padmasaṃbhava buried these texts in the Gampo hills in central Tibet, where later the great teacher Gampopa established his monastery. Many other texts and sacred objects were buried in this way in different places throughout Tibet, and are known as terma, "hidden treasures." Padmasaṃbhava gave the transmission of power to discover the termas to his twenty-five chief disciples. The Bardo texts were later discovered by Karma-Lingpa, who was an incarnation of one of these disciples.

Liberation, in this case, means that whoever comes into contact with this teaching—even in the form of doubt, or with an open mind—receives a sudden glimpse of enlightenment through the power of the transmission contained in these treasures.

Karma-Lingpa belonged to the Nyingma tradition but his students were all of the Kagyü tradition. He gave the first transmission of the six liberation teachings to Dödül-Dorje, the thirteenth Karmapa, who in turn gave it to Gyurme-Tenphel, the eighth Trungpa. This transmission was kept alive in the Surmang monasteries of the Trungpa lineage, and from there it spread back into the Nyingma tradition.

The student of this teaching practices the sādhana and studies the texts so as to become completely familiar with the two maṇḍalas as part of his own experience.

I received this transmission at the age of eight, and was trained in this teaching by my tutors, who also guided me in dealing with dying people. Consequently I visited dying or dead people about four times a week from that time onwards. Such continual contact with the process of death, particularly watching one's close friends and relatives, is considered extremely important for students of this tradition, so that the notion of impermanence becomes a living experience rather than a philosophical view.

This book is a further attempt to make this teaching applicable to students in the West. I hope that the sādhana may also be translated in the near future, so that this tradition may be fully carried out.

CHÖGYAM TRUNGPA, *Rinpoche*

INTRODUCTION

By coincidence, this introduction was written at Rumtek Monastery in Sikkim, looking across the valley to Gangtok where, half a century ago, Kazi Dawa-Samdup translated and W. Y. Evans-Wentz edited the first English version of the *Bardo Thötröl*. A further link with them is provided by the fact that this new translation appeared as part of a series dedicated to Evans-Wentz.

Since their work is so widely known and has been the cause of so much interest in Buddhism, it may be asked why there is any need for a new version. Evans-Wentz himself gives part of the answer in his own Introduction, where he recognizes "the pioneer character of the work." Since then, especially after the flight from Tibet of many of the highest lamas, information about Tibetan Buddhism and interest in it have greatly increased. It is no longer purely a subject of academic study, but a living tradition which is now putting down roots in the West. This makes possible a new approach to translation, in which great importance is given to the practical application of the text, and to conveying its spirit of vitality and directness.

In the summer of 1971 at the Tail of the Tiger Contemplative Community in Vermont (now called Karme-Chöling), Chögyam Trungpa, Rinpoche, gave a seminar entitled *The Tibetan Book of the Dead,* which is included here as a commentary. During the seminar he used a Tibetan text, while the audience followed in the Evans-Wentz edition. Questions about the translation and style of expression continually came up, and as a result of these questions it was decided to prepare a new version.

In making this translation, the Tibetan edition published by E. Kalsang (Varanasi,

1969) was used, together with three block-prints. A few minor omissions and errors have been corrected by reference to the blockprints, but there are no disagreements on any essentials among these four texts. Therefore it is rather surprising to find considerable disagreement with the earlier translation. Without going into great detail, there are a few outstanding points which should be mentioned.

Kazi Dawa-Samdup has several times changed the translation from the original wording, considering it to be mistaken. In the notes the editor quotes the Tibetan texts used—one manuscript and one blockprint—often adding that the translator has corrected certain words which are in error. Most of these alterations seem to have been made in order to reconcile the system of correspondences of deities, symbolic colors, and so on, with those found in other texts. The most striking examples are the following (references are to the paperback edition, Oxford University Press, 1960):

On page 95, note 3, the feminine *Kuntu-Zang-mo* (Samantabhadrī) is changed to the masculine *Kuntu-Zang-po* (Samantabhadra), who thus appears twice. But the whole point of this passage lies in the symbolism of the union of the male and female aspects of mind. As Evans-Wentz himself refers to this in the same note, and again in note 3 on the following page, it is hard to understand how he, or the translator, could have considered the text to be mistaken.

On pages 106 and 109, *matter* (which we translate as "form") and *consciousness* are reversed, so as to make them appear on the first and second days respectively, although in the blockprint they appear the other way round. Similarly, on pages 108 and 111, the consorts *Sangyay-Chanma* (Buddha-Locanā) and *Māmakī* are exchanged.

On page 114, the fourth day, the light

of the pretas (hungry ghosts) is described as red, and on page 117, the fifth day, the light of the asuras (jealous gods) is given as green, while in this version these lights are yellow and red respectively. The colors of the six realms occur again on pages 124 and 174, where Evans-Wentz notes the Tibetan and explains the changes made by the translator to make the colors correspond to the colors of the buddhas.

Buddhist iconography is not absolutely consistent, however. Apparent irregularities such as these occur frequently, always with some reason behind them. In all these cases our four texts agree with Evans-Wentz's blockprint and in most cases also with his manuscript, so it is most likely that such uniformity indicates the correct version.

Other differences between the two translations will be found in the treatment of specifically Buddhist terminology. The original scriptures of Buddhism were written in Sanskrit or Pali (a close derivative of Sanskrit) and were translated into Tibetan from the seventh century onwards. At that time the Tibetan language had not been influenced by any highly developed system of thought, and therefore it could be adapted without too much difficulty; in effect a new philosophical language was created to convey the Buddhist teachings. Translating into a twentieth-century European language presents an entirely different situation. Western thought has developed along very different lines from that of the East, and so if an English word is chosen from the vocabulary of philosophy or religion, it will inevitably contain all kinds of associations and implications which may be quite alien to the underlying assumptions of Buddhism. Conversely, the full range of meaning of a Sanskrit word may not be found in any single English word. In such cases an English equivalent would need just as much explanation as the original, while the Sanskrit word has the advantage of being free from possibly misleading associations in the reader's mind.

Certain terms are therefore kept in Sanskrit, their original language, although the *Bardo Thötröl* was written in Tibetan. The names of deities are also given in Sanskrit, as they are better known in this form and can be more easily identified in other sources. This practice was often followed by the Tibetan translators, although not consistently in this particular text.

It may seem inconsistent to introduce two Tibetan words: *bardo* itself and *yidam*. One reason is simply that these are the easiest words to use, and they have become very familiar to students of Buddhism who will be the main readers of this book. The possible translation of bardo as "intermediate state" is awkward when it is repeated frequently; so is the Sanskrit *antarābhāva*, besides being an unfamiliar term, for this teaching was developed in Tibet rather than in India. *Yidam,* as used in Tibetan Buddhism, has rather different implications from the Sanskrit *iṣṭadevatā,* "chosen deity," familiar in Hinduism. It has been translated as "protective deity" (which should rather be used to describe the dharmapālas) or "tutelary deity," but all these terms seem to convey the idea of an external being, acting as a personal guardian or helper, while the real meaning of yidam is entirely internal and psychological; the yidam is the expression of one's own basic nature, visualized as a divine form in order to relate with it and express its full potentiality.

It is noticeable that several of the words which best express the teachings of Buddhism are part of the language of contemporary psychology, for the attitudes of certain schools of Western psychology often come closer to Buddhism than do those of Western philosophy or religion.

The concept of sin, for instance, is inevitably associated with original sin, guilt, and punishment, which have no place in most Eastern teachings. Instead, Buddhism looks for the basic cause of sin and suffering, and discovers this to be the belief in a self or ego as the center of existence. This belief is caused not by innate evil, but by unconsciousness, or ignorance of the true nature of existence. Since we experience the whole of life from this falsely centralized viewpoint, we cannot know the world as it really is. This is what is meant by saying that the world is unreal. The remedy is to see through the illusion, to attain the insight of emptiness—the absence of what is false. Inseparable from emptiness is the luminosity—the presence of what is real, the basic ground in which the play of life takes place.

Concepts such as conditioning, neurotic patterns of thought and unconscious influences seem more appropriate in this book than conventional religious terms. In the Commentary, words such as neurosis and paranoia are used to describe not pathological conditions but the natural results of this fundamental state of mind. *Projections* indicates the way in which we see things, colored by our own attitudes. In the text, it translates a Tibetan word (*snang*), which basically means "light" or "appearance," whether internal or external, and which Kazi Dawa-Samdup translated as "thought-form" or "vision." "Projection" overcomes this distinction between the subjective and objective.

A very brief outline of the Buddhist psychology relevant to this book may be useful as a basis for the detailed explanations given in the commentary. The evolution of the ego-centered state of being is analyzed in the system of the five skandhas. *Skandha* is literally a heap or group, but its meaning may be better conveyed by "psychological component."

The first component is form (*rūpa*), the beginning of individuality and separate existence, and the division of experience into subject and object. Now there is a primitive "self" aware of an external world. As soon as this happens, the self reacts to its surroundings: this is the second stage, feeling (*vedanā*). It is not yet fully developed emotion—just an instinctive liking, dislike or indifference, but immediately it grows more complicated as the centralized entity asserts itself by reacting not only passively but actively. This is the third stage, perception (*saṃjñā*), in its fullest sense, when the self is aware of stimulus and automatically responds to it. The fourth component is concept (*saṃskāra*), covering the intellectual and emotional activity of interpretation which follows perception. It is what puts things together, and builds up the patterns of personality and karma. Finally there is consciousness (*vijñāna*) which combines all the sense-perceptions and the

...ind. The self has now become a complete universe of its own; instead of directly perceiving the world as it really is, it projects its own images all around it.

The fundamental teaching of this book is the recognition of one's projections and the dissolution of the sense of self in the light of reality. As soon as this is done, these five psychological components of the confused or unenlightened state of mind become instead factors of enlightenment. They are transmuted into their transcendent or purified forms, which are presented during the first five days in the bardo of dharmatā.

During these visionary experiences, the six realms of existence also appear. These are the six main states of the confused mind, and are described in detail in the commentary. Each one appears together with its alternative, the possibility of giving up that particular obsession, ceasing to grasp at the security of a centralized entity, but instead letting oneself dissolve into the corresponding manifestation of wisdom.

These "wisdoms" are the maṇḍalas of the five tathāgatas. Tathāgata literally means "thus-gone," which can be paraphrased as "he who has become one with the essence of what is." It is synonymous with *buddha* ("awakened"), and *jina* ("victorious"). The five tathāgatas, then, are the five chief modes of energy of buddhanature, the fully awakened consciousness. The qualities they embody are the five wisdoms, but in saṃsāra—the world or state of mind in which we live—these energies appear as five poisons or confused emotions. Everything in the world, all living beings, places, events and so on, possesses a predominant characteristic which links it with one of the five; therefore they are also known as the five families.

The first of the tathāgatas, placed in the center of the maṇḍala, is Vairocana. He represents the basic poison of confusion, or ignorance which deliberately ignores, out of which all the others evolve. But he is also the wisdom of the dharmadhātu — the limitless, all-pervading space in which everything exists as it really is. This is the reversal of ignorance. Since he is the original and central figure, his family is simply known as the tathāgata or buddha family, names which again represent the opposite of ignorance.

The second tathāgata is Akṣobhya, in the eastern side of the maṇḍala, which, following Indian tradition, is placed at the bottom. In other texts Akṣobhya may appear at the center, with Vairocana in the east, so there is often some alteration of their attributes; this is why both white and blue colors appear on the first and second days and why there is sometimes an apparent confusion in the maṇḍala pattern. Akṣobhya is the ruler of the vajra family, whose poison is aggression or hatred. This is transmuted into the mirror-like wisdom, which reflects everything calmly and un-critically.

In the southern side of the maṇḍala, drawn to the left, is Ratnasaṃbhava, ruler of the ratna family. *Ratna* means "jewel," and in particular the wish-fulfilling jewel which grants all desires. So here the poison is pride, resulting from possessing riches of whatever kind. Its antidote is the wisdom of equality and equanimity.

Above, in the west, comes Amitābha, whose family is padma, the lotus. He symbolizes passion and desire, grasping hungrily at everything. The wisdom which corresponds to this poison is discrimination, which provides the coolness and detachment for passion to be transformed into compassion.

Lastly, on the right, the northern side, is Amoghasiddhi of the karma family. *Karma* here means "action" and is symbolized by a sword or by a double vajra. Envy is the poison associated with karma, arising from the insatiable ambition which drives this kind of activity, while its enlightened aspect is the wisdom which accomplishes all actions.

The five tathāgatas possess many other attributes, which are described and explained in the commentary. They are also accompanied by their feminine aspects and by bodhisattva emanations.

While the buddhas embody the transcendent qualities of enlightenment existing beyond the flux of life, the bodhisattva principle is one of active engagement for the sake of all beings. The bodhisattvas could be seen as the activity of the five wisdoms. The feminine energy provides the fertile element which completes them and allows their fullest manifestation. These and all the other deities which appear in the book could be described as expressions of the world in the light of reality. They embody the various manifestations of energy which we experience as our whole physical, mental and emotional existence. Although we do not normally perceive our lives in terms of energies, their effects are with us all the time. In his commentary, Trungpa Rinpoche translates them into a language we can recognize more easily—emotions, qualities, environment, ways of life, actions and events.

So, although this book is ostensibly written for the dead, it is in fact about life. The Buddha himself would not discuss what happens after death, because such questions are not useful in the search for reality here and now. But the doctrine of reincarnation, the six kinds of existence, and the intermediate bardo state between them, refer very much to this life, whether or not they also apply after death. It is often emphasized that the purpose of reading the *Bardo Thötröl* to a dead person is to remind him of what he has practiced during his life. This *Book of the Dead* can show us how to live.

COMMENTARY

by Chögyam Trungpa, Rinpoche

THE MESSAGE OF THE BOOK

There seems to be a fundamental problem when we refer to the subject of *The Tibetan Book of the Dead*. The approach of comparing it with *The Egyptian Book of the Dead* in terms of mythology and lore of the dead person seems to miss the point, which is the fundamental principle of birth and death recurring constantly in this life. One could refer to this book as "The Tibetan Book of Birth." The book is not based on death as such, but on a completely different concept of death. It is a "Book of Space." Space contains birth and death; space creates the environment in which to behave, breathe and act, it is the fundamental environment which provides the inspiration for this book.

The pre-Buddhist Bön civilization of Tibet contained very accurate indications on how to treat the psychic force left behind by a dead person, the footprints or temperature, so to speak, which is left behind when he is gone. It seems that both the Bön tradition and the Egyptian are based on that particular type of experience, how to relate with the footprints, rather than dealing with the person's consciousness. But the basic principle I am trying to put across now is that of the uncertainty of sanity and insanity, or confusion and enlightenment, and the possibilities of all sorts of visionary discoveries that happen on the way to sanity or insanity.

Bardo means gap; it is not only the interval of suspension after we die but also suspension in the living situation; death happens in the living situation as well. The bardo experience is part of our basic psychological make-up. There are all kinds of bardo experiences happening to us all the time, experiences of paranoia and uncertainty in everyday life; it is like not being sure of our ground, not knowing quite what we have asked for or what we are getting into. So this book is not only a message for those who are going to die and those who are already dead, but it is also a message for those who are already born; birth and death apply to everybody constantly, at this very moment.

The bardo experience can be seen in terms of the six realms of existence that we go through, the six realms of our psychological states. Then it can be seen in terms of the different deities who approach us, as they are described in the book. In the first week the peaceful deities, and in the last week the wrathful deities; there are the five tathāgatas and the herukas, and the gaurīs, who are messengers of the five tathāgatas, presenting themselves in all sorts of terrifying and revolting fashions. The details presented here are very much what happens in our daily living situation, they are not just psychedelic experiences or visions that appear after death. These experiences can be seen purely in terms of the living situation; that is what we are trying to work on.

In other words, the whole thing is based on another way of looking at the psychological picture of ourselves in terms of a practical meditative situation. Nobody is going to save us, everything is left purely to the individual, the commitment to who we are. Gurus or spiritual friends might instigate that possibility, but fundamentally they have no function.

How do we know that these things actually happen to people who are dying? Has anyone come back from the grave and told us the experiences they went through? Those impressions are so strong that someone recently born should have memories of the period between death and birth; but then as we grow up we are indoctrinated by our parents and society, and we put ourselves into a different framework, so that the original deep impressions become faded except for occasional sudden glimpses. Even then we are so suspicious of such experiences, and so afraid of losing any tangible ground in terms of living in this world, that any intangible kind of experience is treated halfheartedly or dismissed altogether. To look at this process from the point of view of what happens when we die seems like the study of a myth; we need some practical experience of this continual process of bardo.

There is the conflict between body and consciousness, and there is the continual experience of death and birth. There is also the experience of the bardo of dharmatā, the luminosity, and of the bardo of becoming, of possible future parents or grounding situations. We also have the visions of the wrathful and peaceful divinities, which are happening constantly, at this very moment. If we are open and realistic enough to look at it in this way, then the actual experience of death and the bardo state will not be either purely a myth or an extraordinary shock, because we have already worked with it and become familiar with the whole thing.

THE BARDO OF THE MOMENT BEFORE DEATH

The first basic bardo experience is the experience of uncertainty about whether one is actually going to die, in the sense of losing contact with the solid world, or whether one could continue to go on living. This uncertainty is not seen in terms of leaving the body, but purely in terms of losing one's ground; the possibility of stepping out from the real world into an unreal world.

We could say that the real world is that in which we experience pleasure and pain, good and bad. There is some act of intelligence which provides the criteria of things as they are, a basic dualistic notion. But if we are completely in touch with these dualistic feelings, that absolute experience of duality is itself the experience of non-duality. Then there is no problem at all, because duality is seen from a perfectly open and clear point of view in which there is no conflict; there is a tremendous encompassing vision of oneness. Conflict arises because duality is not seen as it is at all. It is seen only in a biased way, a very clumsy way. In fact, we do not perceive anything properly, and we begin to wonder whether such things as myself and my projections really exist. So when we talk about the dualistic world as confusion, that confusion is not the complete dualistic world, but only half-hearted, and this causes tremendous dissatisfaction and uncertainty; it builds up to the point of fear of becoming insane, the point where there are possibilities of leaving the world of duality and going into a sort of woolly, fuzzy emptiness, which is the world of the dead, the graveyard that exists in the midst of fog.

The book describes the death experience in terms of the different elements of the body, going deeper and deeper. Physically you feel heavy when the earth element dissolves into water; and when water dissolves into fire you find that the circulation begins to cease functioning. When fire dissolves into air, any feeling of warmth or growth begins to dissolve; and when air dissolves into space you lose the last feeling of contact with the physical world. Finally, when space or consciousness dissolves into the central nāḍī, there is a sense of internal luminosity, an inner glow, when everything has become completely introverted.

Such experiences happen constantly. The tangible, logical state dissolves, and one is not quite certain whether one is attaining enlightenment or losing one's sanity. Whenever that experience happens it can be seen in four or five different stages. First the tangible quality of physical, living logic becomes vague; in other words, you lose physical contact. Then you automatically take refuge in a more functional situation, which is the water element; you reassure yourself that your mind is still functioning. In the next stage, the mind is not quite sure whether it is functioning properly or not, something begins to cease operating in its circulation. The only way to relate is through emotions, you try to think of someone you love or hate, something very vivid, because the watery quality of the circulation does not work any more, so the fiery temperature of love and hate becomes more important. Even that gradually dissolves into air, and there is a faint experience of openness, so that there is a tendency to lose your grip on concentrating on love or trying to remember the person you love. The whole thing seems to be hollow inside.

The next experience is the luminosity. You are willing to give in because you cannot struggle any more, and a kind of carelessness arises at that moment. It is as though pain and pleasure are occurring at the same time, or a powerful shower of icy cold water and boiling hot water is pouring simultaneously over your body. It is an intense experience, very powerful and full, the experience of oneness where both pain and pleasure are the same. The dualistic struggle of trying to *be* something is completely confused by the two extreme forces of hope for enlightenment and fear of becoming insane. The two extremes are so concentrated that it allows a certain relaxation; and when you do not struggle any more the luminosity presents itself naturally.

The next step is the experience of luminosity in terms of daily life. The luminosity is neutral ground or background, a gap when the intensity slackens. Then some intelligence begins to connect it to the awakened state of mind, leading to a sudden glimpse of meditative experience or buddha nature, which could also be called the dharmakāya. But if we have no means of connecting with the basic intelligence, and confused energy still dominates our process of mind, then the energy builds up blindly and finally falls down into different levels of diluted energy, so to speak, from the absolute energy of the luminosity. Some basic tendency of grasping begins to develop in the state of luminosity, and from that the experience of the six realms of the world develops according to its intensity. But that tenseness or tightness cannot just function by itself without an activator of energy; in other words, energy is being used in order to grasp. We can now look at the six realms of the world from the point of view of different types of instinct.

THE REALM OF HELL

We can begin with the realm of hell, which is the most intense. First there is a build-up of energies, of emotions, to a crescendo, so that at some stage we find it very confusing whether the energies are controlling us or we are controlling them. Then suddenly we lose track of this whole race, and our mind is put into a blank state which is the luminosity. From that blank state an intense temptation to fight begins to develop, and that paranoia also brings terror. Originally the paranoia and terror were supposed to fight against something, but one is not quite certain whom exactly one is fighting; and when the whole thing has developed, the terror begins to turn against oneself. When one tries to strike out, instead of fighting the projection one is striking inward.

It is like the story of the hermit who saw a leg of lamb in front of him, and wanted to pick it up and cook it. His teacher told him to mark it with a cross, then later he discovered that the cross was marked on his own chest. It is that kind of notion; you think there is something outside to attack or fight or win over. In most cases hatred is like that. You are angry with something and try to destroy it, but at the same time the process becomes self-destructive, it turns inward and you would like to run away from it; but then it seems too late, you are the anger itself, so there is nowhere to run away. You are haunting yourself constantly, and that is the development of hell.

Very vivid descriptions of hell are found in Gampopa's *Jewel Ornament of Liberation,* and symbolically each intense torture is a psychological portrait of oneself. In the hell realm you are not exactly punished, but overwhelmed by the environment of terror, which is described as fields and mountains of red-hot iron and space filled with sparks of fire. Even if you decide to run away you have to walk over this burning metal, and if you decide not to run away you are turned into charcoal yourself. There is intense claustrophobia, heat coming from all directions; the whole earth is turned into hot metal, whole rivers are turned into melted iron, and the whole sky is permeated with fire.

The other type of hell is the reverse, the experience of intense cold and snow, an icy world in which everything is completely frozen. This is another type of aggression, the aggression which refuses to communicate at all. It is a kind of indignation which usually comes from intense pride, and the pride turns into an ice-cold environment which reinforced by self-satisfaction begins to get into the system. It does not allow us to dance or smile or hear the music.

THE HUNGRY GHOST REALM

Then we have another realm of mind, that of the pretas or hungry ghosts. To begin with, we get into the luminosity by working up not aggression this time but intense greed. There is a sense of poverty, yet at the same time a sense of richness, contradictory and yet operating together simultaneously.

In the hungry ghost realm there is a tremendous feeling of richness, of gathering a lot of possessions; whatever you want you do not have to look for, but you find yourself possessing it. And this makes us more hungry, more deprived, because we get satisfaction not from possessing alone but from searching. But now, since we have everything already, we cannot go out and look for something and possess it. It is very frustrating, a fundamental insatiable hunger.

It is as though you are completely full, so full that you cannot eat any more; but you love to eat, and so you begin to have hallucinations of the flavor of food and the pleasure of eating it, tasting it, chewing it, swallowing it and digesting it. The whole process seems luxurious, and you feel extremely envious of other people who can really be hungry and eat.

This is symbolized by the image of a

person with a gigantic belly and extremely thin neck and tiny mouth. There are different stages of this experience, depending on the intensity of hunger. Some people can pick food up, but then it dissolves or they cannot eat it; some people can pick it up and put it in their mouth, but they cannot swallow it; and some people can swallow it but once it gets into their stomach it begins to burn. There are all sorts of levels of that hunger, which constantly happen in everyday life.

The joy of possessing does not bring us pleasure anymore once we already possess something, and we are constantly trying to look for more possessions, but it turns out to be the same process all over again; so there is constant intense hunger which is based not on a sense of poverty but on the realization that we already have everything yet we cannot enjoy it. It is the energy there, the act of exchange, that seems to be more exciting; collecting it, holding it, putting it on, or eating it. That kind of energy is a stimulus, but the grasping quality makes it very awkward. Once you hold something you want to possess it, you no longer have the enjoyment of holding it, but you do not want to let go. Again it is a kind of love-hate relationship to projections. It is like the analogy that the next door neighbor's garden is greener; once it becomes ours we realize there is no longer the joy or appreciation of beauty as we saw it at the beginning; the romantic quality of a love affair begins to fade away.

THE ANIMAL REALM

The animal realm is characterized by the absence of sense of humor. We discover that we cannot remain neutral in the luminosity, so we begin to play deaf and dumb, intelligently playing ignorant, which means that one is completely concealing another area, the area of sense of humor. It is symbolized by animals, which cannot laugh or smile; joy and pain are known to animals, but somehow the sense of humor or irony is not known to them.

One could develop this by believing in a certain religious framework, theological or philosophical conclusions, or by just simply remaining secure, practical and solid. Such a person could be very efficient, very good and consistent at work, and quite contented. It is like a country farmer who attends to his farm methodically, with constant awareness and openness and efficiency; or an executive who runs a business; or a family man whose life is very happy, predictable and secure, with no areas of mystery involved at all. If he buys a new gadget there are always directions for using it. If there is any problem he can go to lawyers or priests or policemen, all sorts of professional people who are also secure and comfortable in their professions. It is utterly sensible and predictable, and highly mechanical at the same time.

What is lacking is that if any unknown, unpredictable situation occurs, there is a feeling of paranoia, of being threatened. If there are people who do not work, who look different, whose whole life-style is irregular, then the very existence of such people is in itself threatening. Anything unpredictable fundamentally threatens the basic pattern. So that apparently sane and solid situation without sense of humor is the animal realm.

THE HUMAN REALM

The human realm brings out another kind of situation which is not quite the same as the animal realm of surviving and living life. The human realm is based on passion, the tendency to explore and enjoy; it is the area of research and development, constantly trying to enrich. One could say that the human realm is closer psychologically

to the hungry ghost quality of striving for
something, but it also has some element of
the animal realm, of putting everything
into action predictably. And there is something extra connected with the human
realm, a very strange kind of suspicion
which comes with passion, and which
makes human beings more cunning, shifty
and slippery. They can invent all sorts of
tools and accentuate them in all sorts of
sophisticated ways so as to catch another
slippery person, and the other slippery
person develops his or her own equipment
of anti-tools. So we build up our world
with tremendous success and achievement,
but this escalation of building up tools and
anti-tools develops constantly, and intro-
duces more sources of passion and intrigue. Finally we are unable to accomplish
such a big undertaking. We are subject to
birth and death. The experience can be

born, but it can also die; our discoveries may be impermanent and temporary.

THE REALM OF THE JEALOUS GODS

The realm of the asuras or jealous gods is the highest realm as far as communication goes, it is a very intelligent situation. When you are suddenly separated from the luminosity there is a feeling of bewilderment, as though someone had dropped you in the middle of a wilderness; there is a tendency to look back and suspect your own shadow, whether it is a real shadow or someone's strategy. Paranoia is a kind of radar system, the most efficient radar system the ego could have. It picks up all sorts of faint and tiny objects, suspecting each one of them, and every experience in life is regarded as something threatening.

This is known as the realm of jealousy or envy, but it is not envy or jealousy as we generally think of them. It is something extremely fundamental, based on survival and winning. Unlike the human or animal realm, the purpose of this realm of the jealous gods is purely to function within the realm of intrigue; that is all there is, it is both occupation and entertainment. It is as if a person were born a diplomat, raised as a diplomat, and died as a diplomat. Intrigue and relationship are his life-style and his whole livelihood. This intrigue could be based on any kind of relationship, an emotional relationship, or the relationship between friends, or the relationship of teacher and student, whatever there may be.

THE REALM OF THE GODS

The final stage is the realm of the gods, deva-loka. Again, when the person awakes from or steps out of the luminosity, there is some kind of unexpected pleasure, and one wants to maintain that pleasure. Instead of completely dissolving into neutral ground one suddenly begins to realize one's individuality, and individuality brings a sense of responsibility, of maintaining oneself. That maintaining oneself is the state of samādhi, perpetually living in a state of absorption and peace; it is the realm of the gods, which is known as the realm of pride. Pride in the sense of building one's own centralized body, preserving one's own health; in other words, it is intoxication with the existence of ego. You begin to feel thankful to have such confirmation that you *are* something after all, instead of the luminosity which is no man's land. And because you *are* something, you have to maintain yourself, which brings a natural state of comfort and pleasure, complete absorption into oneself.

These six realms of the world are the source of the whole theme of living in saṃsāra, and also of stepping into the dharmakāya realm. This will help us to understand the significance of the visions described in the book of the bardo of becoming, which is another kind of world. There is a confrontation of these two worlds: the experience of the six realms from the point of view of ego, and from the point of view of transcending ego. These visions could be seen as expressions of neutral energy, rather than as gods to save you from saṃsāra or demons to haunt you.

THE BARDO OF DHARMATĀ

Along with the six realms, we should have some understanding of the basic idea of bardo: *bar* means in between, and *do* means island or mark; a sort of landmark which stands between two things. It is rather like an island in the midst of a lake. The concept of bardo is based on the period between sanity and insanity, or the period between confusion and the confusion just about to be transformed into wisdom; and of course it could be said of the experience which stands between death and birth. The past situation has just occurred and the future situation has not yet manifested itself so there is a gap between the two. This is basically the bardo experience.

The dharmatā bardo is the experience of luminosity. Dharmatā means the essence of things as they are, the is-ness quality. So the dharmatā bardo is basic, open, neutral ground, and the perception of that ground is dharmakāya, the body of truth or law.

When the perceiver or activator begins to dissolve into basic space, then that basic space contains the dharma, contains the truth, but that truth is transmitted in terms of saṃsāra. So the space between saṃsāra and the truth, the space the dharma comes through, provides the basic ground for the details of the five tathāgatas and the peaceful and wrathful visions.

These expressions of the dharmatā are manifested not in physical or visual terms but in terms of energy, energy which has the quality of the elements, earth, water, fire, air, and space. We are not talking about ordinary substances, the gross level of the elements, but of subtle elements. From the perceiver's point of view, perceiving the five tathāgatas in the visions is not vision and not perception, not quite experience. It is not vision, because if you have vision you have to look, and looking is in itself an extroverted way of separating yourself from the vision. You cannot perceive, because once you begin to perceive you are introducing that experience into your system, which means again a dualistic style of relationship. You cannot even know it, because as long as there is a watcher to tell you that these are your experiences, you are still separating those energies away from you. It is very important to understand this basic principle, for it is really the key point of all the iconographical symbolism in tantric art. The popular explanation is that these pictures of different divnities are psychological portraits, but there is something more to it than this.

One of the most highly advanced and dangerous forms of practice is the bardo retreat, which consists of seven weeks of meditation in utter darkness. There are very simple visualizations, largely based on the principle of the five tathāgatas seen as different types of eyes. The central place of the peaceful tathāgatas is in the heart, so you see the different types of eyes in your heart; and the principle of the wrathful divinities is centralized in the brain, so you see certain types of eyes gazing at each other within your brain. These are not ordinary visualizations, but they arise out of the possibility of insanity and of losing ground altogether to the dharmatā principle.

Then an absolute and definite experience of luminosity develops. It flashes on and off; sometimes you experience it, and sometimes you do not experience it but you are in it, so there is a journey between dharmakāya and luminosity. Generally around the fifth week there comes a basic understanding of the five tathāgatas, and these visions actually happen, not in terms of art at all. One is not exactly aware of their presence, but an abstract quality begins to develop, purely based on energy. When energy becomes independent, complete energy, it begins to look at itself and perceive itself, which transcends the ordinary idea of perception. It is as though you walk because you know you do not need any support; you walk unconsciously. It is that kind of independent energy without any self-consciousness, which is not at all fantasy—but then again, at the same time, one never knows.

THE NATURE OF THE VISIONS

The visions that develop in the bardo state, and the brilliant colors and sounds that come along with the visions, are not made out of any kind of substance which needs maintenance from the point of view of the perceiver, but they just happen, as expression of silence and expression of emptiness. In order to perceive them properly, the perceiver of these visions cannot have fundamental, centralized ego. Fundamental ego in this case is that which causes one to meditate or perceive something.

If there were a definite perceiver, one could have a revelation of a god or external entity, and that perception could extend almost as far as a non-dualistic level. Such perception becomes very blissful and pleasant, because there is not only the watcher but also something more subtle, a basic spiritual entity, a subtle concept or impulse, which looks outward. It begins to perceive a beautiful idea of wideness and openness and blissfulness, which invites the notion of oneness with the universe. This feeling of the openness and wideness of the cosmos could become very easy and comfortable to get into. It is like returning to the womb, a kind of security. Because of the inspiration of such union, the person becomes loving and kind naturally, and speaks in beautiful language. Quite possibly some form of divine vision could be perceived in such a state, or flashes of light or music playing, or some presence approaching.

In the case of such a person who relates to himself and his projections in that way, it is possible that in the after death period of the bardo state he might be extremely

irritated to see the visions of the tathāgatas, which are not dependent on his perception. The visions of the tathāgatas do
not ask for union at all, they are terribly
hostile; they are just there, irritatingly
there because they will not react to any
attempts to communicate.

The first vision that appears is the vision
of the peaceful divinities; not peacefulness
in the sense of the love and light experience we have just been talking about, but
of completely encompassing peace, immovable, invincible peace, the peaceful
state that cannot be challenged, that has
no age, no end, no beginning. The symbol
of peace is represented in the shape of a
circle; it has no entrance, it is eternal.

Not only in the bardo experience after
death alone, but also during our lifetime,
similar experiences occur constantly.
When a person is dwelling on that kind of
union with the cosmos—everything is

beautiful and peaceful and loving—there is the possibility of some other element coming in, exactly the same as the vision of the peaceful divinities. You discover that there is a possibility of losing your ground, losing the whole union completely, losing your identity as yourself, and dissolving into an utterly and completely harmonious situation, which is, of course, the experience of the luminosity. This state of absolute peacefulness seems to be extremely frightening, and there is often the possibility that one's faith might be shaken by such a sudden glimpse of another dimension, where even the concept of union is not applicable any more.

There is also the experience of the wrathful divinities. They are another expression of peacefulness, the ruthless, unyielding quality, not allowing sidetracks of any kind. If you approach them and try to reshape the situation they throw you back.

That is the kind of thing that continually happens with emotions in the living situation. Somehow the feeling of unity where everything is peaceful and harmonious does not hold final truth, because whenever there is a sudden eruption of energies in terms of passion or aggression or any conflict, suddenly something wakes you up; that is the wrathful quality of the peacefulness. When you are involved in ego-manufactured, comforting situations of any kind, the actual reality of the nakedness of mind and the colorful aspect of emotions will wake you up, possibly in a very violent way, as a sudden accident or sudden chaos.

Of course there is always the possibility of ignoring these reminders and continuing to believe the original idea. So the concept of leaving the body and entering the luminosity, then waking up from the luminosity and perceiving these visions in the third bardo state could be seen symbolically as being delivered into that open space — space without even a body to relate to, such open space that you cannot have the notion of union because there is nothing to be united with or by. But there are flashes of energy floating, which could be either diverted or channeled in; that is the definition of mind in this case, the gullible energy which could be diverted into another situation or turned into a rightful one. The possibility of freeing oneself into the sambhogakāya level of the five tathāgata realms depends on whether or not there is any attempt to go on playing the same game constantly.

At the same time as these vivid and colorful experiences, there is also the playing back of the six realms of the bardo experience. The perception of the six realms and the perception of the five tathāgatas are one state, but they have different styles. It seems that the perceiver of the tathāgatas, this kind of mind, has tremendous ability to keep the link between physical body and mind, very spontaneously. There is no division between the spirituality of the mind and the spirituality of the body; they are both the same, so there is no conflict.

The book says that the first time you awaken from the unconscious absorption in the body, you have a visual experience, minute and precise and clear, luminous and terrifying, rather like seeing a mirage in a spring field, and also you hear a sound which is like a thousand thunders roaring simultaneously. In the mental state there is a looseness and detached feeling, while at the same time overloaded with intelligence, as though the person had a head without a body, a gigantic head floating in space. So the actual visual experience of this bardo state, the preparation for perceiving the visions of the tathāgatas, is clear and intelligent and luminous, but at the same time intangible, not knowing where you are exactly; and that sensual experience is also happening in the audible sphere, a deep sound roaring in the background, earth-shaking, but at the same time there is nothing to vibrate. Similar experiences can also happen in life, although the absence of a physical body makes the bardo experience more clear and more hallucinatory. In a life situation there is not the extreme aspect of the mirage, but there is a basically desolate quality, loneliness and flickering, when the person begins to realize that there is no background area to relate to as ego. That sudden glimpse of egolessness brings a kind of shakiness.

THE FIRST DAY

It says in this book that having woken up, after four days of unconsciousness, into the luminosity there is a sudden understanding that this is the bardo state, and at that very moment the reverse of saṃsāric experience occurs. This is the perception of light and images, which are the reverse of body or form; instead of being a tangible situation of form it is an intangible state of quality.

Then you get the dazzling light, which is a link of communication between body and intelligence. Although one is absorbed into the state of luminosity, there is still some intelligence operating, sharp and precise, with a dazzling quality. So the psychophysical body and also the intelligence, the intellectual mind, are transformed into space.

In this case the color of space is blue, and the vision that appears is Vairocana.

Vairocana is described as the buddha who has no back and front; he is panoramic vision, all-pervading with no centralized notion. So Vairocana is often personified as a meditating figure with four faces, simultaneously perceiving all directions. He is white in color, because that perception does not need any other tinge, it is just the primordial color, white. He is holding a wheel with eight spokes, which represents transcending the concepts of direction and time. The whole symbolism of Vairocana is the decentralized notion of panoramic vision; both center and fringe are everywhere. It is complete openness of consciousness, transcending the skandha of consciousness.

Along with that there is a vision of the realm of the gods. The depth of the blue is terrifying because there is no center to hold on to, but the glimpse of the white light is like seeing a lamp burning in darkness, and one tends to walk towards it.

The realm of the gods also happens in our daily life experiences. Whenever we are absorbed in a spiritual state, a trance-like state of joy and pleasure, involved in our own self and its projections, whenever that joy comes there is also the possibility of its opposite, the centerless, all-pervading quality of Vairocana. It is extremely irritating, not at all attractive because there is nothing to indulge in, no basic ground in which we can enjoy ourselves. It is all very well to have a panoramic vision of openness, but if there is no one to perceive it, it is terrible from the point of view of ego. The contract between the realm of the gods and Vairocana constantly happens in life, and often the choice is left to us, whether we should cling to a centralized source of spiritual pleasure, or whether we should let go into pure openness without a center.

This experience comes from aggression, because aggression holds us back and keeps us away from seeing Vairocana. Aggression is a definite, solid thing; when we are in a state of complete anger it is like imagining ourselves to be a porcupine, putting out everything possible to protect ourselves. There is no room for panoramic vision; we do not want to have four faces at all, we hardly even want to have one eye. It is very centralized and completely introverted, that is why anger might make us run away from the expansive quality of Vairocana.

THE SECOND DAY

Transcending the water element, the white light begins to dawn, and in the east, the Realm of Complete Joy, the tathāgata Vajrasattva or Akṣobhya appears.

Akṣobhya means immovable, and *Vajra-sattva* means vajra being; they both indicate toughness, solidity. In Indian mythology vajra is the most precious jewel, or the thunderbolt, which destroys all other weapons and jewels, which can cut diamond. There was a certain sage who meditated on Mount Meru for centuries, and when he died his bones were transformed into vajra, and Indra, the king of the gods, discovered this and made his weapon out of it, a vajra with a hundred points. The vajra has three qualities: it can never be used frivolously, it always fulfills its function of destroying the enemy, and it always returns into your hand. It is indestructible, adamantine.

The tathāgata Vajrasattva-Akṣobhya is holding a five-pointed vajra—this absolutely solid object, and he is sitting on an elephant throne—what could be more solid than that? His consort is Buddha-

Locanā, the Buddha Eye. In the Buddhist tradition there are five types of eyes: the bodily eye, the buddha eye, the wisdom eye, the heavenly eye and the dharma eye. In this case the buddha eye refers to awakening. You may have a very solid, stable situation, but if you have no outlet it can stagnate. The feminine principle automatically opens out, she provides the exit or activation of the whole thing, the element of communication from solidness into a flowing, living situation.

He is accompanied by the bodhisattva Kṣitigarbha, the Essence of Earth, who represents any kind of fertility and growth, also an expression of that particular buddha. And he is also accompanied by Maitreya, the Loving One. That firmness, solid and fertile at the same time, needs emotion as well in order to give life to the solidity; it is the emotional, compassionate quality of love, not necessarily selfless compassion.

Then there are the female bodhisattvas: Lāsyā is the bodhisattva of dance or mudrā, she is more performer than dancer, the offering goddess who displays the beauty and dignity of the body; she shows the majesty and seductiveness of the feminine principle. And Puṣpā is the goddess of flowers, the bodhisattva of vision, sight, the scenery.

Transcending the skandha of form are mirrorlike rays, white and glittering, clear and precise, which shine from the heart of Vajrasattva and his consort. Along with that there is the light of hell, grey light without brilliance. When the person perceives such a display of the vajra quality it seems too complicated to work with, so there is a possibility of simplifying it into the grey light, associated with hell or a fundamental notion of paranoia which is always connected with the intellectual vajra quality. In order to have intellectual understanding you have to see what is wrong with everything rather than what is right; that is the natural vajra intellectual quality, the critical attitude of the logical mind, which also brings solidity. If you have an understanding of something founded on the logic of a critical attitude, then your wisdom is based on extremely solid and definite ground; it is unshakable. But the other aspect of it is the realm of hell, when the critical attitude does not relate to solidity or basic sanity of any kind, but sets off a chain reaction, an alarm clock so to speak, of paranoia.

THE THIRD DAY

In the process of this sequence of days, the dharmadhātu quality of Vairocana has provided space, and the quality of Vajrasattva-Akṣobhya has provided solidity. Now the vision of Ratnasaṃbhava is described. Ratnasaṃbhava is the central figure of the ratna family, which consists of richness and dignity, the expansion of wealth into other areas, fundamentally solid, rich and expansive. The negative aspect of ratna quality is taking advantage of richness in order to march into other territories, expanding into whatever space exists, over-emphasizing generosity to the point where there is a blockage of communication.

Ratnasaṃbhava is yellow in color, which represents the earth; fertility in the sense of wealth and richness. He is holding the wish-fulfilling gem, which also means the absence of poverty. And Māmakī, his consort, represents water; in order to have rich, fertile soil the earth needs water.

The bodhisattva Ākāśagarbha is the Essence of Space. With such rich ground you also need space to create perspective. And there is Samantabhadra, the All-Good, who is the basic strength, the organic quality of the whole maṇḍala of the ratna family. According to the traditional way of finding appropriate locations to build a home or a monastery or cultivate a new field (which was quite possibly developed by the Bön tradition of Tibet), you do not build a house merely at random, but there are psychological factors involved. There should be the open feeling of the east, and the luscious feeling of the south with brooks and rivers, and the fortifying feeling of the west with rocks, and the protective feeling of the north with its mountain ranges. There is also a way of water divining by looking at the shape of the land, and next to the spring of water there is usually a spot which is not swampy but has a good rocky foundation to build a house. That particular rocky substance, surrounded by such appropriate shapes and locations, is called Samantabhadra, the soil Samantabhadra. Samantabhadra is also associated with aspiration and positive thinking, a basic confidence and positive way of looking at the future.

Ratnasambhava is accompanied by the female bodhisattva Mālā, the goddess who offers all sorts of adornments, garlands, necklaces, bracelets and so on, to bring out the highlights of the earthy quality of ratna. The other female bodhisattva is Dhūpā, the goddess who carries incense. She represents smell, scent, the environmental situation that earth creates; the fresh air, air without pollution, and the room for vegetation to grow and rivers to run.

The light associated with the ratna family is the yellow light of equanimity, nondiscriminating light. But it seems as though all that detail and richness of the ratna maṇḍala is too elaborate, too majestic, so there is a possibility that one would rather run into a very simple and self-satisfied little corner, and that little area is pride, the dim light of the human world.

THE FOURTH DAY

On the fourth day there is the purified element of fire, represented by Amitābha, the padma family. Amitābha means boundless light, and the basic quality of padma is magnetizing, seductive, invitingly warm, open and compassionate. The light is boundless because it just shines naturally, it does not ask for any reward. It has the nature of fire, not in the sense of aggression, but of consuming any substance without rejecting or accepting.

He is holding a lotus in his hand, which means the same thing: the lotus opens when the sun or the moon shines on it, it opens towards the light, so any situation coming from outside is accepted. It also has the quality of complete purity; such compassion could grow in mud or dirt but the flower is completely perfect and clean. Sitting on a peacock seat is again openness and acceptance; in mythology the peacock is supposed to be fed on poison, and its beautiful colors are formed from eating poison. It is openness which extends so far that it can deal with any kind of negative situation, in fact compassion is exhilarated by negative situations.

His consort Pāṇḍaravāsinī, the White-clad One, is associated with the symbolism of an Indian legend of certain clothes woven from stone, which could only be cleaned by fire. She represents the essence of fire, consuming everything, and also the result of the consuming process, purification, complete compassion.

Then there is the bodhisattva Avaloki-teśvara, the essence of compassion, he who sees in all directions, which is the ultimate intelligence of compassion. Whenever compassion is needed it happens naturally, it has a sharp, automatic quality; it is not idiot or blind compassion, but intelligent compassion which always fulfills its function. Mañjuśrī too represents the mechanical aspect of compassion, but here it is an intellectual rather than a purely impulsive quality. He is also the creator of sound, the communication of compassion; he represents the sound of emptiness which is the source of all words.

Then there is Gītā, the female bodhisattva of song, who sings to the music of Mañjuśrī; and along with her is Ālokā, who holds a lamp or torch. The whole process of compassion has rhythm and light, it has the depth of intelligence and the sharpness of efficiency, and it has the purifying nature of the white-clad buddha as well as the infinite, all-pervading quality of Amitābha.

That is the complete padma family,

which transcends the skandha of perception and shines with the red light of discriminating awareness wisdom. Compassion is very detailed and precise, so it is necessary to have discriminating awareness wisdom, which does not mean discriminating in terms of acceptance and rejection, but simply seeing things as they are.

In this book it is associated with the realm of the hungry ghosts; there is some conflict here, because passion is usually connected with the human realm. All these padma qualities, sharpness and precision and depth and majesty, have been found too overwhelming, and somehow one would like to play a game of deaf and dumb; one would like to sneak away from that complete picture into the sidetracks of ordinary passions.

THE FIFTH DAY

On the fifth day there is the karma family, which is the pure quality of air or wind. It is a green light; the color of envy. From the Realm of Accumulated Actions the tathāgata Amoghasiddhi appears. The karma family is associated with action and fulfillment and efficiency. It is powerful and nothing can stand in its way, therefore it is regarded as destructive. Amoghasiddhi means accomplishing all actions, all powers.

He is holding a crossed vajra in his hand. The vajra is a symbol of fulfilling all actions, tough and indestructible, as we saw in the vajra family. The crossed vajra represents the area of all activities completely perceived in all directions, panoramic fulfillment; often it is described as a multicolored vajra.

He is sitting on a seat of shang-shang, a kind of garuḍa; this particular type of garuḍa is a musician, he holds two cymbals in his hands and plays them as he carries Amoghasiddhi on his back. It is again a very powerful image and a symbol of ful-fillment, a kind of superbird, a transcen-dental bird who can fly and cover all areas, encompassing all space.

His consort is Samaya-Tārā, the Savior of Sacred Word or Samaya. There are dif-ferent interpretations of samaya in the tan-tric teachings, but in this case it is the ac-tual fulfillment of the living situation at that moment.

Then there is the bodhisattva Vajrapāṇi, which means the Vajra-holder. Again it symbolizes tremendous energy; he is the bodhisattva of energy. And also Sarvanivar-aṇaviskambhin, the Purifier of all Hin-drances. If any hindrance happens in the process of karmic action, it comes from misunderstanding or inability to be in con-tact with the actual living situation, so the bodhisattva clears away these hindrances. In other words, this karma family contains both the absence of any hindrance, and the power of fulfillment.

Then there are the female bodhisattvas Gandhā and Naivedyā. Gandhā is the bodhisattva of perfume, she carries essence made out of all sorts of herbs, which represents the sense-perceptions or feelings; in order to have efficient skillful activity you need developed sense-perception. Naivedyā offers food, the food of meditation which nourishes skillful action.

The karma family transcends the skandha of concept, and is connected with the realm of the jealous gods. Again, as in any experience of wisdom as opposed to confusion, they both have the same quality. In this case they both have the quality of occupation, but wisdom completely covers the ground of all possibilities, seeing all possible ways of dealing with the situation in terms of subject and object, energy, texture, temperament, speed, space and so on, whereas confusion has a very limited way of dealing with situations, because it has never expanded itself or developed at all. Confusion is underdeveloped wisdom, primitive wisdom, while wisdom is completely developed.

THE SIXTH DAY

Next there is a crescendo of all the forty-two peaceful divinities. The five tathāgatas, the four guardians of the gates, the four goddesses and the six realms of the world appear simultaneously. We have a situation of basic bewilderment within which the five tathāgatas fill up all the space, all the directions, as well as any corners of emotional situations; there is no gap, no escape or sidetrack of any kind, because the four gates are also guarded by the four types of herukas.

The eastern gatekeeper is known as the Victorious One, which is connected with pacifying, but he appears in a wrathful form to provide an awe-inspiring situation at the gate, so that you do not even think of getting out. He represents the indestructible, invincible quality of peace, that is why he is victorious.

Then the second one, in the southern gate, is the Enemy of Yama the Lord of Death. He is associated with the karmic activity of increasing wealth. Wealth in terms of time and space is very limited, rationed, so he who goes beyond that limitation is the Lord of the Lord of Death.

In the western gate is the Horse-headed Hayagrīva. He is the equivalent of an alarm system, as the neigh of the horse can wake you up in any unprepared situations. It is connected with magnetizing, which is a kind of intelligent passion, so that you do not get involved in passion but it wakes you up.

In the northern gate is Amṛtakuṇḍalī, the Coil of Amṛta or anti-death potion. He is particularly associated with death. If there is any suicidal impulse of giving up hope, the anti-death medicine revives you; suicide is not the answer at all. You have the peaceful presence of victory, the increasing one which conquers any extreme concept of time and space, the magnetizing principle which sends out an alarm, and the suicidal principle which gives you the anti-death potion. Fundamentally you are completely locked in without any sidetracks.

Moreover, there are the female principles of the gatekeepers. There is the female principle with a hook, to catch you like a fish if you try to run away. Or if you try to escape in terms of pride, to fill up all the space and not allow any other possibilities, the goddess with a lasso ties you from head to toe leaving you without any chance to expand. Another possibility is to run away through passion which is based on speed, but then the goddess with the chain chains you down so that you cannot move your feet and run away. And if you try to frighten anybody by aggression and make your way out, then the goddess with a very loud bell subdues your loud scream of aggression and your deep voice of anger.

Then you are reduced to facing the six realms of the world: the buddha of the gods, the buddha of the jealous gods, the buddha of the human beings, the buddha of the animals, the buddha of the hungry ghosts and the buddha of the hell realm. All these visions appear from your heart center, which is associated with emotion, passion and pleasure.

THE SEVENTH DAY

Next, the vidyādharas begin to shine out from the throat center, which is the essence of the communication principle. The peaceful divinities are associated with the heart, and the wrathful divinities with the brain. Speech is the link of communication between the two, which is the vidyādharas. *Vidyādhara* means holder of knowledge or insight. They are not quite peaceful and not quite wrathful, but intermediary; they are impressive, overpowering, majestic. They represent the divine form of the tantric guru, possessing power over the magical aspects of the universe.

At the same time, the green light of the animal realm appears, symbolizing ignorance which needs the teaching of the guru to enlighten it.

THE WRATHFUL DEITIES

Now the principles of the five tathāgatas are transformed into the herukas and their consorts. The basic qualities of the families continue, but now they are expressed in a very dramatic, theatrical way; this is the energy of vajra, padma, and so on, rather than just their basic qualities. The herukas have three heads and six arms. The symbolical meaning behind this is the power of transmutation, expressed in the mythical story of the subjugation of Rudra.

Rudra is someone who has achieved complete egohood. There were two friends studying under a teacher, and their teacher said that the essence of his teaching was spontaneous wisdom; even if a person were to indulge himself in extreme actions, they would become like clouds in the sky and be freed by fundamental spontaneity. The two disciples understood it entirely differently. One of them went away and began to work on the spontaneous way of relating to his own characteristics, positive and negative, and became able to free them spontaneously without forcing anything, neither encouraging nor suppressing them. The other one went away and built a brothel, and organized a big gang of his friends who all acted in a spontaneous way, making raids on the nearby villages, killing the men and carrying off the women.

After some time they met again, and both were shocked by each other's kind of spontaneity, so they decided to go and see their teacher. They both presented their experience to him, and he told the first that his was the right way, and the second that his was the wrong way. But the second friend could not bear to see that all his effort and energy had been condemned, so he drew a sword and killed the teacher on the spot. When he himself died he had a succession of incarnations, five hundred as scorpions, five hundred as jackals and so on, and eventually he was born in the realm of the gods as Rudra.

He was born with three heads and six arms, with fully grown teeth and nails. His mother died as soon as he was born, and the gods were so horrified that they took both him and the body of his mother to a charnel ground and put them in a tomb. The baby survived by sucking his mother's blood and eating her flesh, so he became very terrifying and healthy and powerful. He roamed around the charnel ground, and began to control all the local ghosts and deities and create his own kingdom just as before, until he had conquered the whole threefold universe.

At that time his former teacher and his fellow student had already attained enlightenment, and they thought they should

try to subjugate him. So Vajrapāṇi manifested himself as Hayagrīva, a wrathful red
figure with a horse's head, and uttered
three neighs to proclaim his existence in
the kingdom of Rudra. Then he entered
Rudra's body by his anus, and Rudra was
extremely humiliated; he acknowledged
his subjugation and offered his body as a
seat or a vehicle. All the attributes of
Rudra and the details of his royal costume,
the skull crown, skull cup, bone orna-
ments, tiger-skin shirt, human-skin shawl
and elephant-skin shawl, armor, pair of
wings, crescent moon in his hair, and so
on, were transmuted into the heruka costume.

First there is the Great Heruka who is
not associated with any of the five families,
he is the space between the five families.
The Great Heruka creates the basic energy
of all the wrathful herukas, and then come
the Buddha Heruka, Vajra Heruka, Ratna

Heruka, Padma Heruka and Karma Heruka with their respective consorts. They represent the outrageous, exuberant quality of energy which cannot be challenged. Fundamentally the quality of the five families is a peaceful state, open and passive, because it is completely stable and nothing can disturb it; the tremendous power of that peaceful state manifests as wrathful. It is often described as compassionate anger, anger without hatred.

Then there are the gaurīs, another type of wrathful energy. The five herukas are the existence of energy as it is, while the gaurīs are activating energy. The white gaurī dances on a corpse, her activity is to extinguish thought processes, therefore she holds a mace of a baby's corpse. Generally a corpse symbolizes the fundamental neutral state of being; a body without life is the state without any active thoughts, good or bad, the nondualistic state of mind. Then the yellow goddess holds a bow and arrow because she has achieved the unity of skillful means and knowledge; her function is to bring them together. And then there is the red gaurī holding a banner of victory made out of the skin of a sea-monster. The sea-monster symbolizes the principle of saṃsāra, which cannot be escaped; the goddess holding it as a banner means that saṃsāra is not rejected but accepted as it is. Then in the north is Vetālī, black in color, holding a vajra and a skull cup because she symbolizes the unchanging quality of dharmatā. The vajra is indestructible, and the skull cup is another symbol of skillful means. We do not have to go through all of them in detail, but just to give a basic idea of these gaurīs and messengers connected with the wrathful maṇḍala, each particular figure has a function in fulfilling a particular energy.

The wrathful deities represent hope,

and the peaceful deities represent fear. Fear in the sense of irritation, because the ego cannot manipulate them in any way; they are utterly invincible, they never fight back. The hopeful quality of wrathful energy is hope in the sense of a perpetual creative situation, seen as it really is, as basic neutral energy which continues constantly, belonging neither to good nor bad. The situation may seem overwhelming and beyond your control, but there is really no question of controlling or being controlled. The tendency is to panic, to think you can keep control; it is like suddenly realizing that you are driving very fast, so you put the brake on, which causes an accident. The gaurīs' function is to come between body and mind. Mind in this case is the intelligence, and body is the impulsive quality, like panicking, which is a physical action. The gaurīs intervene between intelligence and action, they cut the continuity of the self-preservation of the ego; that is their wrathful quality. They transmute destructive energy into creative energy. Just as the body of Rudra was transformed into the heruka, so the force behind the impulsive quality of panic or action is transmuted.

THE DYING PERSON

It seems that in the Tibetan culture people do not find death a particularly irritating or difficult situation, but here in the West we often find it extremely difficult to relate to it. Nobody tells us the final truth. It is such a terrible rejection, a fundamental rejection of love, that nobody is really willing to help a dying person's state of mind.

It seems necessary, unless the dying person is in a coma or cannot communicate, that he should be told he is dying. It may be difficult to actually take such a step, but if one is a friend or a husband or wife, then this is the greatest opportunity of really communicating trust. It is a delightful situation, that at last somebody really cares about you, somebody is not playing a game of hypocrisy, is not going to tell you a lie in order to please you, which is what has been happening throughout your whole life. This comes down to the ultimate truth, it is fundamental trust, which is extremely beautiful. We should really try to generate that principle.

Actually relating with the dying person is very important, telling him that death is not a myth at that point, but that it is actually happening. "It is actually happening, but we are your friends, therefore we are watching your death. We know that you are dying and you know that you are dying, we are really meeting together at this point." That is the finest and best demonstration of friendship and communication, it presents tremendously rich inspiration to the dying person.

You should be able to relate with his bodily situation, and detect the subtle deterioration in his physical senses, sense of communication, sense of hearing, facial expression and so on. But there are people with tremendously powerful will who can always put on a smile up to the last minute of death, trying to fight off their old age, trying to fight the deterioration of their senses, so one should be aware of that situation also.

Just reading the *Bardo Thötröl* does not do very much, except that the dying person knows that you are performing a ceremony of some kind for him. You should have some understanding of the whole thing, not just reading out of the book but making it like a conversation: "You are dying, you are leaving your friends and family, your favorite surroundings will no longer be there, you are going to leave us. But at the same time there is something which continues, there is the continuity of your positive relationship with your friends and with the teaching, so work on that basic continuity, which has nothing to do with the ego. When you die you will have all sorts of traumatic experiences, of leaving the body, as well as your old memories coming back to you as hallucinations. Whatever the visions and hallucinations may be, just relate to what is happening rather than trying to run away. Keep there, just relate with that."

While you are doing all this, the intelligence and consciousness of the dying person are deteriorating, but at the same time he also develops a higher consciousness of the environmental feeling; so if you are able to provide a basic warmth and a basic confidence that what you are telling him is the truth rather than just what you have been told to tell him, that is very important.

It should be possible to give some kind of simple explanation of the process of deterioration from earth into water, water into fire and so on, this gradual deterioration of the body, finally ending up in the luminosity principle. In order to bring the person into a state of luminosity you need the basic ground to relate with it, and this basic ground is the solidity of the person. "Your friends know you are going to die, but they are not frightened by it, they are really here, they are telling you that you are going to die, there is nothing suspicious going on behind your back." Fully being there is very important when a person dies. Just relating with nowness is extremely powerful, because at that point there is uncertainty between the body and the mind. The body and brain are deteriorating, but you are relating with that situation, providing some solid ground.

As far as the visions of the peaceful and wrathful divinities are concerned, it seems to be very much left to the individual to relate with them himself. In the book it says that you should try to conjure up the spirit of the dead person and tell him about the images; you may be able to do that if there is still continuity, but it is very much guesswork as far as ordinary people are concerned; there is no real proof that you have not lost touch with the person. The whole point is that when you instruct a dying person you are really talking to yourself. Your stability is part of the dying person, so if you are stable then automatically the person in the bardo state will be attracted to that. In other words, present a very sane and solid situation to the person who is going to die. Just relate with

him, just open to each other simultaneously, and develop the meeting of the two
minds.

THE TIBETAN BOOK
OF THE DEAD

Homage to the Gurus, the three Kāyas:
Amitābha, Infinite Light,
 the Dharmakāya,
Peaceful and Wrathful Lotus Deities,
 the Saṃbhogakāya,
Padmasaṃbhava, Protector of Beings,
 the Nirmāṇakāya. ⸭[1]

This "Great Liberation through Hearing," the means of liberation in the bardo for yogins of average capacities, is in three parts: the introduction, the main subject-matter, and the conclusion. ⸭

Firstly the introduction, the means of liberating human beings. First of all one should have studied the instructions, which should certainly liberate those of the highest capacities; but if they do not one should practice the ejection of consciousness,[2] which liberates spontaneously as soon as it is thought of, in the bardo of the moment before death. This should certainly liberate yogins of average capacities, but if it does not one should strive in this "Great Liberation through Hearing" in the bardo of dharmatā.⸫

Therefore the yogin should first examine the sequence of the signs of death according to the "Spontaneous Liberation of the Signs of Death," and when they are definitely completed he should effect the ejection of consciousness, which liberates spontaneously as soon as it is thought of. If ejection is effected there is no need to read the "Liberation through Hearing," but if not it should be read clearly and precisely, close to the dead body.⸫

If the body is not present, one should sit on the dead person's bed or seat, and proclaiming the power of truth call on his consciousness and read, imagining him sitting in front listening. At this time sounds of crying and weeping are not good, so his relatives should be shut out. If the body is present, then during the interval between the ceasing of the breath and the ceasing of pulsation in the arteries, his guru or a dharma-brother or a dharma-sister[3] whom he loved and trusted should read this "Great Liberation through Hearing" close to his ear. ∹

The teaching of the "Liberation through Hearing." An elaborate offering should be made to the Three Jewels[4] if the materials are available, but if they are not available one should set out whatever there is and visualize the rest without limit. One should say the "Inspiration-Prayer Calling on the Buddhas and Bodhisattvas for Rescue" seven or three times, then loudly recite the "Inspiration-Prayer for Deliverance from the Dangerous Pathway of the Bardo" and the "Main Verses of the Bardo." Then read "The Great Liberation through Hearing" seven or three times. ∹

It is in three parts: showing the luminosity in the bardo of the moment before death, the great reminder of showing in the bardo of dharmatā, and the instructions for closing the entrance to the womb in the bardo of becoming.⁝

First, showing the luminosity in the bardo of the moment before death. By having this read to them, all kinds of ordinary people, who have received teaching but have not recognized although they are intelligent, or who have recognized but have practiced little, will recognize the basic luminosity and bypass the bardo experience to reach the unoriginated dharmakāya.⁝

The method of instruction: it is best if his principal guru from whom he requested teaching can be present, but otherwise a dharma-brother or dharma-sister with whom he has taken the samaya vow, or a spiritual friend in the same lineage. If none of these are to be found, then someone who can read aloud clearly and precisely should read it several times. This will remind him of what his guru has shown him and he will immediately recognize the basic luminosity and be liberated, there is no doubt.⸭

The time of instruction: when respiration has ceased, prāṇa is absorbed into the wisdom-dhūtī, and luminosity free from complexities shines clearly in the consciousness. If prāṇa is reversed and escapes into the right and left nāḍīs, the bardo state appears suddenly, so the reading should take place before the prāṇa escapes into the right and left nāḍīs. The length of time during which the inner pulsation remains after respiration has ceased is just about the time taken to eat a meal.⸭

The method of instruction: it is best if ejection of consciousness is effected when the respiration is just about to stop, but if it has not been effected one should say these words:⸭

"O child of noble family, (name), now the time has come for you to seek a path. As soon as your breath stops, what is called the basic luminosity of the first bardo, which your guru has already shown you, will appear to you. This is the dharmatā, open and empty like space, luminous void, pure naked mind without center or circumference. Recognize then, and rest in that state, and I too will show you at the same time." ⦂

This should be firmly implanted in his mind by repeating it many times over in his ear until he stops breathing. Then, when the ceasing of the breath is heard, one should lay him down on the right side in the lion position[5] and firmly press the two pulsating arteries, which induce sleep, until they have stopped throbbing. Then the prāṇa which has entered the dhūtī will not be able to go back and will be certain to emerge through the brahmarandhra. ⦂

Now the showing should be read. At this time the first bardo, which is called the luminosity of dharmatā, the undistorted mind of the dharmakāya, arises in

82

the mind of all beings. Ordinary people call this state unconscious because the prāṇa sinks into the avadhūtī during the interval between the ceasing of the breath and of the pulsation. The time it lasts is uncertain, depending on the spiritual condition and the stage of yogic training. It lasts for a long time in those who have practiced much, were steady in the meditation practice of tranquillity, and sensitive. In striving to show such a person one should repeat the instruction until pus comes out from the apertures of his body. In wicked and insensitive people it does not last longer than a single snapping of the fingers, but in some it lasts for the time taken to eat a meal. As most sūtras and tantras say that this unconscious state lasts for four and a half days, generally one should strive to show the luminosity for that length of time. ⸪

The method of instruction: If he is able, he will work with himself from the instructions already given. But if he cannot by himself, then his guru, or a disciple of his guru, or a dharma-brother or dharma-sister who was a close friend, should stay nearby and read aloud clearly the sequence of the signs of death: "Now the sign of earth dissolving into water is present, water into fire, fire into air, air into consciousness. . . ." When the sequences is almost completed he should be encouraged to adopt an attitude like this, "O child of noble family," or, if he was a guru, "O Sir," — "do not let your thoughts wander." This should be spoken softly in his ear. In the case of a dharma-brother, a dharma-sister, or anyone else, one should call him by name and say these words:÷

"O child of noble family, that which is called death has now arrived, so you should adopt this attitude: 'I have arrived at the time of death, so now, by means of this death, I will adopt only the attitude of the enlightened state of mind, friendliness and compassion, and attain perfect enlightenment for the sake of all sentient beings as limitless as space. With this attitude, at this special time for the sake of all sentient beings, I will recognize the luminosity of death as the dharmakāya, and attaining in that state the supreme realization of the Great Symbol,[6] I will act for the good of all beings. If I do not attain this, I will recognize the bardo state as it is, and attaining the indivisible Great Symbol form in the bardo, I will act for the good of all beings as limitless as space in whatever way will influence them.' Without letting go of this attitude you should remember and practice whatever meditation teaching you have received in the past."⁂

These words should be spoken distinctly with the lips close to his ear, so as to remind him of his practice without letting his attention wander even for a moment. Then, when respiration has completely stopped, one should firmly press the arteries of sleep and remind him with these words, if he was a guru or spiritual friend higher than oneself:⸭

"Sir, now the basic luminosity is shining before you; recognize it, and rest in the practice."⸭

And one should show all others like this:⸭

"O child of noble family, (name), listen. Now the pure luminosity of the dharmatā is shining before you; recognize it. O child of noble family, at this moment your state of mind is by nature pure emptiness, it does not possess any nature whatever, neither substance nor quality such as color, but it is pure emptiness; this is the dharmatā, the female buddha Samantabhadrī. But this state of mind is not just blank emptiness, it is unobstructed, sparkling, pure and vibrant; this mind is the male buddha Samantabhadra.[7] These two, your mind whose nature is emptiness without any substance whatever, and your mind

which is vibrant and luminous, are inseparable: this is the dharmakāya of the buddha. This mind of yours is inseparable luminosity and emptiness in the form of a
great mass of light, it has no birth or
death, therefore it is the buddha of Im-
mortal Light. To recognize this is all that
is necessary. When you recognize this
pure nature of your mind as the buddha,
looking into your own mind is resting in
the buddha-mind."÷

This should be repeated three or seven
times, clearly and precisely. Firstly, it will
remind him of what he has previously been
shown by his guru; secondly, he will recognize his own naked mind as the luminosity; and thirdly, having recognized himself, he will become inseparably united
with the dharmakāya and certainly attain
liberation.÷

If he recognizes the first luminosity he
will be liberated. But if it is feared that he
has not recognized the first luminosity,

then what is called the second luminosity will shine, and that comes when a little more than the time taken to eat a meal has passed after the respiration has ceased. ؞

According to good or bad karma, the prāṇa escapes into the right or left nāḍī, and comes out through the apertures of the body, and the consciousness suddenly becomes clear. To say that this lasts for the time taken to eat a meal depends on whether he is sensitive or insensitive and on whether or not he has practiced. Then his consciousness emerges and he does not know whether he is dead or not. He will see his relatives gathered there just as before, and hear their cries. ؞

During this time, when the violent confused projections of karma have not yet appeared, and the terrors of the Lords of Death have not yet come, the instructions should be given. Here there is a distinction between the perfection stage and the generation stage.[8] If he was working on the perfection stage, one should call his name three times and repeat the instructions given above for showing the luminosity. If he was working on the generation stage, one should read aloud the sādhana and description of his yidam,[9] and remind him with these words: "O child of noble family, meditate on your yidam and do not be distracted. Concentrate intensely on your yidam. Visualize him as an appearance without substance of its own, like the moon in water; do not visualize him as having a solid form." If he is an ordinary person, one should show him by saying: "Meditate on the Lord of Great Compassion."⁑

There is no doubt that those who have not recognized the bardo will grasp it by being shown in this way. But those who were not adept in meditation, even if they were shown by their guru while they were alive, will not be able to clarify the bardo state by themselves, so that their guru, a dharma-brother or a dharma-sister must make it clear. And it is necessary for someone to instruct those who cannot remember during the bardo of the moment before death because they were confused by serious illness, even though they were adept in meditation. It is also extremely necessary for those who, although they were formerly adept in meditation on this path, may enter into lower existences because they have broken the precepts or because their samaya practice has degenerated. ⸱

It is best if he understands during the first bardo, but if he has not understood his insight is awakened by the reminder in the second bardo, and he will be liberated. During the second bardo, his consciousness, which did not know whether he was dead or not, suddenly becomes clear; this is called the pure illusory body. If he understands the teaching at this time, the mother and son dharmatās meet, and he is no longer dominated by karma. Just as the light of the sun overcomes darkness, so the power of karma is overcome by the luminosity of the path, and liberation is attained. This, which is called the second bardo, flashes before the mental body, and the consciousness is able to hear again just as before. If this instruction is understood at this time, its purpose is fulfilled, and since the confused projections of karma have not yet appeared, he is able to direct himself anywhere. ⁝

In this way he is liberated by recognizing the luminosity during the second bardo, even if he did not recognize the basic luminosity. But if he is not liberated by it, then what is called the third bardo, the bardo of dharmatā, arises. The confused projections of karma will appear in the third bardo, so it is most important that the great showing of the bardo of dharmatā is read at this time, for it is very powerful and helpful. ⁝

At this time his relatives are crying and weeping, his share of food is stopped, his clothes are removed, his bed is taken to pieces, and so on. He can see them but they cannot see him, and he can hear them calling him but they cannot hear him calling them, so he goes away in despair. Three phenomena will appear at this time: sounds, colored lights and rays of light, and he will grow faint with fear, terror and bewilderment, so at this moment the great showing of the bardo of dharmatā should be read. Calling the dead person by name, one should say these words very distinctly:⁝

"O child of noble family, listen carefully without distraction. There are six bardo states: the bardo of birth, the bardo of dreams, the bardo of samādhi-meditation, the bardo of the moment before death, the bardo of dharmatā and the bardo of becoming. O child of noble family, you will experience three bardo states: the bardo of the moment before death, the bardo of dharmatā and the bardo of becoming. Of these three, the luminosity of dharmatā in the bardo of the moment before death shone until yesterday, but you did not recognize it, and so you had to wander here. Now you will experience the bardo of dharmatā and the bardo of becoming, so recognize what I will show you without distraction.⁖

"O child of noble family, now what is called death has arrived. You are not alone in leaving this world, it happens to everyone, so do not feel desire and yearning for this life. Even if you feel desire and yearning you cannot stay, you can only wander in saṃsāra. Do not desire, do not yearn. Remember the Three Jewels. O child of noble family, whatever terrifying projections appear in the bardo of dharmatā, do not forget these words, but go forward remembering their meaning; the essential point is to recognize with them:⁖

Now when the bardo of dharmatā dawns
    upon me,
I will abandon all thoughts of fear and
    terror,
I will recognize whatever appears as my
    projection
and know it to be a vision of the bardo;
now that I have reached this crucial point
I will not fear the peaceful and wrathful
    ones, my own projections. ⁝

"Go forward, saying these words clearly and distinctly, and remembering their meaning. Do not forget them, for the essential point is to recognize with certainty that whatever appears, however terrifying, is your own projection. ⁝

"O child of noble family, when your body and mind separate, the dharmatā will appear, pure and clear yet hard to discern, luminous and brilliant, with terrifying brightness, shimmering like a mirage on a plain in spring. Do not be afraid of it, do not be bewildered. This is the natural radiance of your own dharmatā, therefore recognize it.⸪

"A great roar of thunder will come from within the light, the natural sound of dharmatā, like a thousand thunderclaps simultaneously. This is the natural sound of your own dharmatā, so do not be afraid or bewildered. You have what is called a mental body of unconscious tendencies, you have no physical body of flesh and blood, so whatever sounds, colors and rays of light occur, they cannot hurt you and you cannot die. It is enough simply to recognize them as your projections. Know this to be the bardo state.⸪

"O child of noble family, if you do not recognize them in this way as your projections, whatever meditation practice you have done during your life, if you have not met with this teaching, the colored lights will frighten you, the sounds will bewilder you and the rays of light will terrify you. If you do not understand this essential point of the teaching you will not recognize the sounds, lights and rays, and so you will wander in saṃsāra. ⁑

"O child of noble family, after being unconscious for four and a half days you will move on, and awakening from your faint you will wonder what has happened to you, so recognize it as the bardo state. At that time, saṃsāra is reversed, and everything you see appears as lights and images. ⁑

"The whole of space will shine with a blue light, and Blessed Vairocana will appear before you from the central Realm, All-pervading Circle. His body is white in color, he sits on a lion throne, holding an eight-spoked wheel in his hand and embracing his consort the Queen of Vajra Space. The blue light of the skandha of consciousness in its basic purity, the wisdom of the dharmadhātu, luminous, clear, sharp and brilliant, will come towards you from the heart of Vairocana and his consort, and pierce you so that your eyes cannot bear it. At the same time, together with it, the soft white light of the gods will also come towards you and pierce you. At that time, under the influence of bad karma, you will be terrified and escape from the wisdom of the dharmadhātu with its bright blue light, but you will feel an emotion of pleasure towards the soft white light of the gods. At that moment do not be frightened or bewildered by the luminous, brilliant, very sharp and clear blue light of supreme wisdom, for it is the light-ray of the buddha, which is called the wisdom of the dharmadhātu. Be drawn to it with faith and devotion, and supplicate it, thinking, 'It is the light-ray of Blessed Vairocana's compassion, I take refuge in it.' It is Blessed Vairocana coming to invite you in the dangerous pathway of the bardo; it is the light-ray of Vairocana's compassion. ፥

"Do not take pleasure in the soft white light of the gods, do not be attracted to it or yearn for it. If you are attracted to it you will wander into the realm of the gods and circle among the six kinds of existence. It is an obstacle blocking the path of liberation, so do not look at it, but feel longing for the bright blue light, and repeat this inspiration-prayer after me with intense concentration on Blessed Vairocana: ፥

> When through intense ignorance I
>   wander in saṃsāra,
> on the luminous light-path of the
>   dharmadhātu wisdom,
> may Blessed Vairocana go before me,
> his consort the Queen of Vajra Space
>   behind me;

help me to cross the bardo's
dangerous pathway
and bring me to the perfect
buddha state." ⸭

By saying this inspiration-prayer with deep devotion, he will dissolve into rainbow light in the heart of Blessed Vairocana and his consort, and become a saṃbhoga-kāya buddha in the central Realm, the Densely Arrayed. ⸭

But if, even after being shown, he is afraid of the lights and the rays because of his aggression and neurotic veils, and he escapes, and if he is confused even after saying the prayer, then on the second day Vajrasattva's circle of deities will come to invite him, together with his bad karma which leads to hell. So, to show him, one should call the dead person by name and say these words: ⸭

"O child of noble family, listen without distraction. On the second day, a white light, the purified element of water, will shine, and at the same time Blessed Vajra-sattva-Akṣobhya will appear before you from the blue eastern Realm of Complete Joy. His body is blue in color, he holds a five-pointed vajra in his hand and sits on an elephant throne, embracing his consort Buddha-Locanā. He is accompanied by the two male bodhisattvas Kṣitigarbha and Maitreya and the two female bodhisattvas[10] Lāsyā and Puṣpā, so that six buddha forms appear. ÷

"The white light of the skandha of form in its basic purity, the mirror-like wisdom, dazzling white, luminous and clear, will come towards you from the heart of Vajrasattva and his consort and pierce you so that your eyes cannot bear to look at it. At the same time, together with the wisdom light, the soft smoky light of hell-beings will also come towards you and pierce you. At that time, under the influence of aggression, you will be terrified and escape from the brilliant white light, but you will feel an emotion of pleasure towards the soft smoky light of the hell-beings. At that moment do not be afraid of the sharp, brilliant, luminous and clear white light, but recognize it as wisdom. Be drawn to it with faith and longing, and supplicate it, thinking, 'It is the light-ray of Blessed Vajrasattva's compassion, I take refuge in it.' It is Blessed Vajrasattva coming to invite you in the terrors of the bardo; it is the light-ray hook of Vajrasattva's compassion, so feel longing for it. ⁝

"Do not take pleasure in the soft smoky light of the hell-beings. This is the inviting path of the veils of error, accumulated by your violent aggression. If you are attracted to it will fall down into hell, and sink into the muddy swamp of unbearable suffering from which there is never any escape. It is an obstacle blocking the path of liberation, so do not look at it, but give up aggression. Do not be attracted to it, do not yearn for it. Feel longing for the luminous, brilliant, white light, and say this inspiration-prayer with intense concentration on Blessed Vajrasattva: ❖

> *When through intense aggression*
>   *I wander in saṃsāra,*
> *on the luminous light-path of the*
>   *mirror-like wisdom,*
> *may Blessed Vajrasattva go before me,*
> *his consort Buddha-Locanā behind me;*
> *help me to cross the bardo's dangerous*
>   *pathway*
> *and bring me to the perfect*
>   *buddha state.''* ❖

By saying this inspiration-prayer with deep devotion, he will dissolve into rainbow light in the heart of Blessed Vajrasattva, and become a saṃbhogakāya buddha in the eastern Realm of Complete Joy. ❖

Yet even after being shown in this way, some people are afraid of the light-ray hook of compassion, because of their pride and veils of error, and they escape. So then on the third day Blessed Ratnasaṃbhava's circle of deities will come to invite them, together with the light-path to the human realm. So to show him again, one should call the dead person by name and say these words:

"O child of noble family, listen without distraction. On the third day, a yellow light, the purified element of earth, will shine, and at the same time Blessed Ratnasaṃbhava will appear before you from the yellow southern Realm, The Glorious. His body is yellow in color, he holds a wish-fulfilling jewel in his hand and sits on a horse throne, embracing his consort Māmakī. He is accompanied by the two male bodhisattvas Ākāśagarbha and Samantabhadra and the two female bodhisattvas

Mālā and Dhūpā, so that six buddha forms appear out of the space of rainbow light.⁝

"The yellow light of the skandha of feeling in its basic purity, the wisdom of equality, brilliant yellow, adorned with discs of light, luminous and clear, unbearable to the eyes, will come towards you from the heart of Ratnasambhava and his consort and pierce your heart so that your eyes cannot bear to look at it. At the same time, together with the wisdom light, the soft blue light of human beings will also pierce your heart. At that time, under the influence of pride, you will be terrified and escape from the sharp, clear yellow light, but you will feel an emotion of pleasure and attraction towards the soft blue light of human beings. At that moment do not be afraid of the yellow light, luminous and clear, sharp and bright, but recognize it as wisdom. Let your mind rest in it, relaxed, in a state of nonaction, and be drawn to it with longing. If you recognize it as the natural radiance of your own mind, even though you do not feel devotion and do not say the inspiration-prayer, all the forms and lights and rays will merge inseparably with you, and you will attain enlightenment. If you cannot recognize it as the natural radiance of your own mind, supplicate it with devotion, thinking, 'It is the light-ray of Blessed Ratnasambhava's compassion, I take refuge in it.' It is the light-ray hook of Blessed Ratnasambhava's compassion, so feel longing for it. ⸪

"Do not take pleasure in the soft blue light of human beings. That is the inviting light-path of unconscious tendencies, accumulated by your intense pride. If you are attracted to it you will fall into the human realm and experience birth, old age, death and suffering, and never escape from the muddy swamp of saṃsāra. It is an obstacle blocking the path of liberation, so do not look at it, but give up pride, give up your unconscious tendencies. Do not be attracted to it, do not yearn for it. Feel longing for the luminous, brilliant yellow light, and say this inspiration-prayer with intense one-pointed concentration on Blessed Ratnasambhava: ⸙

> *When through intense pride*
> *I wander in saṃsāra,*
> *on the luminous light-path of*
> *the wisdom of equality,*
> *may Blessed Ratnasambhava go*
> *before me,*
> *his consort Māmakī behind me;*
> *help me to cross the bardo's*
> *dangerous pathway*
> *and bring me to the perfect*
> *buddha state."* ⸙

By saying this inspiration-prayer with deep devotion, he will dissolve into rainbow light in the heart of Blessed Ratna-

sambhava and his consort, and become a
sambhogakāya buddha in the southern
Realm, The Glorious. ⸪

By being shown in this way liberation is
certain, however weak one's capacities may
be. Yet even after being shown like this
many times, there are people whose good
opportunities have run out, such as those
who have done great evil or let their samaya practice degenerate, who will not
recognize. Disturbed by desire and the
veils of error, they will be afraid of the
sounds and lights and will escape, so then
on the fourth day Blessed Amitābha's circle of deities will come to invite them, together with the light-path of the hungry
ghosts, built from desire and meanness. To
show him again, one should call the dead
person by name and say these words: ⸪

"O child of noble family, listen without
distraction. On the fourth day, a red light,
the purified element of fire, will shine, and

at the same time Blessed Amitābha will appear before you from the red western Realm, The Blissful. His body is red in color, he holds a lotus in his hand and sits on a peacock throne, embracing his consort Pāṇḍaravāsinī. He is accompanied by the two male bodhisattvas Avalokiteśvara and Mañjuśrī and the two female bodhisattvas Gītā and Ālokā, so that six buddha forms appear out of the space of rainbow light. ⁝

"The red light of the skandha of perception in its basic purity, the wisdom of discrimination, brilliant red, adorned with discs of light, luminous and clear, sharp and bright, will come from the heart of Amitābha and his consort and pierce your heart so that your eyes cannot bear to look at it. Do not be afraid of it. At the same time, together with the wisdom light, the soft yellow light of the hungry ghosts will also shine. Do not take pleasure in it; give up desire and yearning.⸭

"At that time, under the influence of intense desire, you will be terrified and escape from the sharp, bright red light, but you will feel pleasure and attraction towards the soft yellow light of the hungry ghosts. At that moment do not fear the red light, sharp and brilliant, luminous and clear, but recognize it as wisdom. Let your mind rest on it, relaxed, in a state of non-action. Be drawn to it with faith and longing. If you recognize it as your own natural radiance, even if you do not feel devotion and do not say the inspiration-prayer, all the forms and lights and rays will merge inseparably with you, and you will attain enlightenment. If you cannot recognize it in this way, supplicate it with devotion, thinking, 'It is the light-ray of Blessed Amitābha's compassion, I take refuge in it.' It is the light-ray hook of Blessed Amitābha's compassion. Feel devotion and do not escape. Even if you escape it will stay with you inseparably.⚬

"Do not be afraid, do not be attracted to the soft yellow light of the hungry ghosts. That is the light-path of unconscious tendencies accumulated by your intense desire. If you are attracted to it you will fall into the realm of hungry ghosts, and experience unbearable misery from hunger and thirst. It is an obstacle blocking the path of liberation, so do not be attracted to it, but give up your unconscious tendencies. Do not yearn for it. Feel longing for the luminous, brilliant red light, and say this inspiration-prayer with intense one-pointed concentration on Blessed Amitābha and his consort:⚬

> *When through intense desire*
> *I wander in saṃsāra,*
> *on the luminous light-path*
> *of discriminating wisdom,*

may Blessed Amitābha go before me,
his consort Pāṇḍaravāsinī behind me;
help me to cross the bardo's
    dangerous pathway
and bring me to the perfect
    buddha state." ❖

By saying this inspiration-prayer with deep devotion, he will dissolve into rainbow light in the heart of Blessed Amitābha, Infinite Light, with his consort, and become a saṃbhogakāya buddha in the western Realm, The Blissful. ❖

It is impossible not to be liberated by this, yet even after being shown in this way, sentient beings cannot give up their unconscious tendencies because of long habituation, and under the influence of envy and evil karma they are afraid of the sounds and lights; they are not caught by the light-ray hook of compassion, but wander downwards to the fifth day of the bardo state. So then Blessed Amoghasiddhi's circle of deities with their light-rays of compassion will come to invite them, and the light-path of the jealous gods, built from the emotion of envy, will also invite them. Then, to show him again, one should call the dead person by name and say these words: ÷

"O child of noble family, listen without distraction. On the fifth day, a green light, the purified element of air, will shine, and at the same time Blessed Amoghasiddhi, lord of the circle, will appear before you from the green northern Realm, Accumulated Actions. His body is green in color, he holds a double vajra in his hand and sits on a throne of shang-shang birds soaring in the sky, embracing his consort Samaya-Tārā. He is accompanied by the two male bodhisattvas Vajrapāṇi and Sarvanivaraṇa-viskambhin and the two female bodhisattvas Gandhā and Naivedyā, so that six buddha forms appear out of the space of rainbow light. ⁘

"The green light of the skandha of concept in its basic purity, the action-accomplishing wisdom, brilliant green, luminous and clear, sharp and terrifying, adorned with discs of light, will come from the heart of Amoghasiddhi and his consort and pierce your heart so that your eyes cannot bear to look at it. Do not be afraid of it. It is the spontaneous play of your own mind, so rest in the supreme state free from activity and care, in which there is no near or far, love or hate. At the same time, together with the wisdom light, the soft red light of the jealous gods, caused by envy, will also shine on you. Meditate so that there is no difference between love and hate. But if your intelligence is weak, then simply do not take pleasure in it. ⁘

"At that time, under the influence of intense envy, you will be terrified and escape from the sharp, brilliant green light, but you will feel pleasure and attraction towards the soft red light of the jealous gods. At that moment do not be afraid of the green light, sharp and brilliant, luminous and clear, but recognize it as wisdom. Let your mind rest in it, relaxed, in a state of nonaction, and supplicate it with devotion, thinking, 'It is the light-ray of Blessed Amoghasiddhi's compassion, I take refuge in it.' It is the light-ray hook of Blessed Amoghasiddhi's compassion, called the action-accomplishing wisdom, so long for it and do not escape. Even if you escape it will stay with you inseparably.

"Do not be afraid of it, do not be attracted to the soft red light of the jealous gods. That is the inviting path of karma accumulated by your intense envy. If you are attracted to it you will fall into the realm of the jealous gods, and experience unbearable misery from fighting and quarreling. It is an obstacle blocking the path of liberation, so do not be attracted to it, but give up your unconscious tendencies. Feel longing for the luminous, brilliant green light, and say this inspiration-prayer with intense one-pointed concentration on Blessed Amoghasiddhi and his consort:

> *When through intense envy I wander*
> *   in saṃsāra,*
> *on the luminous light-path of action-*
> *   accomplishing wisdom,*
> *may Blessed Amoghasiddhi go before me,*
> *his consort Samaya-Tārā behind me;*
> *help me to cross the bardo's*
> *   dangerous pathway*
> *and bring me to the perfect*
> *   buddha state."*

By saying this inspiration-prayer with deep devotion, he will dissolve into rainbow light in the heart of Blessed Amoghasiddhi and his consort, and become a saṃbhogakāya buddha in the northern Realm, Perfected Actions. ⁙

However weak his good karmic results may be, by being shown like this in many stages, if he does not recognize at one he will at another, so it is impossible not to be liberated. But even after being shown in this way many times, those who have been habituated to many unconscious tendencies for a long time and have never become familiar with the pure visions of the five wisdoms, are carried backwards by their bad tendencies even though they are shown, so that they are not caught by the light-ray hook of compassion, but become bewildered and frightened by the lights and rays, and wander downwards. So then on the sixth day the buddhas of the five families with their consorts and attendant deities will appear simultaneously, and at the same time the lights of the six realms will also shine simultaneously. ⁙

To show him, one should call the dead person by name and say these words:❖

"O child of noble family, listen without distraction. Even though you were shown when the light of each of the five families appeared until yesterday, under the influence of bad tendencies you were bewildered by them, and so you have remained here until now. If you had recognized the natural radiance of the wisdoms of those five families as your own projection, you would have dissolved into rainbow light in the body of one of the five families and become a saṃbhogakāya buddha, but because you did not recognize you have gone on wandering here until this time. So now watch without distraction.❖

"Now the five families will appear all together, and what is called the four wisdoms combined will come to invite you; recognize them. O child of noble family, the four colored lights of the four purified elements will shine; at the same time the buddha Vairocana and his consort will appear just as before from the central Realm, All-pervading Circle; the buddha Vajrasattva with his consort and attendants will appear from the eastern Realm, Complete Joy; the buddha Ratnasaṃbhava with his consort and attendants will appear from the southern Realm, The Glorious; the buddha Amitābha with his consort and attendants will appear from the western Blissful Realm of Lotuses; and the buddha Amoghasiddhi with his consort and attendants will appear from the northern Realm, Perfected Actions, out of the space of rainbow light. ⸭

"O child of noble family, beyond those buddhas of the five families the wrathful guardians of the gates will also appear: Vijaya, the Victorious; Yamāntaka, Destroyer of Death; Hayagrīva, the Horse-necked; and Amṛtakuṇḍalī, Coil of Nectar; and the female guardians of the gates: Aṅkuśā, the Hook; Pāśā, the Noose; Śṛṅkhalā, the Chain; and Ghaṇṭā, the Bell. The six sages, the Blessed Ones, will also appear: Indra of the hundred sacrifices, sage of the gods; Vemacitra, Splendid Robe, sage of the jealous gods; the Lion of the Śākyas, sage of human beings; Dhruvasiṅha, Steadfast Lion, sage of the animals; Jvālamukha, Flaming Mouth, sage of the hungry ghosts; and Dharmarāja, the Dharma King, sage of the hell-beings. Samantabhadra and Samantabhadrī, the All-Good Father and Mother of all the buddhas, will also appear. These forty-two deities of the sambhogakāya will emerge from within your own heart and appear before you; they are the pure form of your projections, so recognize them. ⁂

"O child of noble family, those realms too do not exist anywhere else, but lie in the four directions of your heart with the center as fifth, and now they emerge from within your heart and appear before you. Those images too do not come from anywhere else, but are the primordial spontaneous play of your mind, so recognize them in this way. O child of noble family, those images are neither large nor small, but perfectly proportioned. They each have their own adornments, their costume, their color, their posture, their throne and their symbol. They are spread out in five couples; each of the five is encircled by a halo of the five colored lights. The whole mandala, the male and female deities of the families, will appear completely, all at once. Recognize them, for they are your yidams. ❖

"O child of noble family, from the hearts of those buddhas of the five families and their consorts, the light-rays of the four wisdoms will each shine upon your heart, very fine and clear, like sunbeams stretched out.⁝

"First the wisdom of the dharmadhātu, a cloth of luminous white light-rays, brilliant and terrifying, will shine upon your heart from the heart of Vairocana. In this cloth of light-rays a sparkling white disc will appear, very clear and bright, like a mirror facing downwards, adorned with five discs like itself, ornamented with discs and smaller discs, so that it has no center or circumference.⁝

"From the heart of Vajrasattva, on the luminous blue cloth of the mirrorlike wisdom, will appear a blue disc like a turquoise bowl face-downwards, adorned with discs and smaller discs.⁝

"From the heart of Ratnasaṃbhava, on the luminous yellow cloth of the wisdom of equality, will appear a yellow disc like a golden bowl face-downwards, adorned with discs and smaller discs.⁝

"From the heart of Amitābha, on the luminous red cloth of the wisdom of discrimination, will appear a sparkling red disc like a coral bowl face-downwards, shining with the deep light of wisdom, very clear and bright, adorned with five discs like itself, ornamented with discs and smaller discs, so that it has no center or circumference. ⁝

"They too will shine upon your heart. ⁝

"O child of noble family, these also have arisen out of the spontaneous play of your own mind, they have not come from anywhere else; so do not be attracted to them, do not fear them, but stay relaxed in a state free from thought. In that state all the images and light-rays will merge with you and you will attain enlightenment. ⁝

"O child of noble family, the green light of action-accomplishing wisdom does not appear, because the energy of your wisdom is not yet fully matured. ⁝

"O child of noble family, this is called the experience of the four wisdoms combined, the passage-way of Vajrasattva. At this time, remember your guru's previous teachings on the showing. If you remember the meaning of the showing you will have faith in your earlier experiences, and so you will recognize them, like the meeting of mother and son or like seeing old friends again. As though cutting off doubt, you will recognize your own projections and enter the pure, changeless path of the dharmatā; and through that faith a continuous meditative state will arise, and you will dissolve into the great self-existing form of wisdom and become a saṃbhoga-kāya buddha who never falls back.⁑

"O child of noble family, together with the wisdom lights, the lights of the impure, illusory six realms will shine: the soft white light of the gods, the soft red light of the jealous gods, the soft blue light of human beings, the soft green light of the animals, the soft yellow light of the hungry ghosts and the soft smoky light of hell-beings. These six will shine together with the pure wisdom lights. At that moment do not grasp or be attracted to any of them, but stay relaxed in a state free from thought. If you are afraid of the pure wisdom lights and attracted to the impure lights of the six realms, you will take on the body of a creature of the six realms, and you will grow weary, for there is never any escape from the great ocean of the misery of saṃsāra. ⸭

"O child of noble family, if you have not been shown by a guru's instruction you will be afraid of those images and pure wisdom lights, and attracted to the impure lights of saṃsāra; do not do so, but feel devotion to the pure wisdom lights, sharp and brilliant. Think with devotion, 'The light-rays of the wisdom and compassion of the Blessed Ones, the buddhas of the five families, have come to seize me with compassion; I take refuge in them.' Do not be attracted to the lights of the six realms of illusion, do not yearn for them, but say this inspiration-prayer with intense one-pointed concentration on the buddhas of the five families and their consorts: ⁝

> When through the five poisons
>   I wander in saṃsāra,
> on the luminous light-path of
>   the four wisdoms combined,
> may the conquerors, the five families,
>   go before me,
> the consorts of the five families
>   behind me;
> save me from the light-paths of
>   the six impure realms,
> help me to cross the bardo's
>   dangerous pathway
> and bring me to the five pure
>   buddha-realms.'' ⁝

By saying this inspiration-prayer, the superior person recognizes his own projections, and merging with non-duality becomes a buddha; the average person recognizes himself through intense devotion and attains liberation; even the inferior person prevents rebirth in the six realms by the purifying power of the prayer, and understanding the meaning of the four wisdoms combined, attains enlightenment by the passage-way of Vajrasattva. By being shown clearly and precisely in this way, many sentient beings will recognize and be liberated. ⁑

But some, such as inferior people in uncivilized places, and wicked people who have no experience of dharma at all, and those who have let their samaya practice degenerate, are confused by their karma, and do not recognize even when they are shown, but wander downwards. So, on the seventh day, the vidyādharas will come from the Pure Realm of Space to invite them, and at the same time the light-path of the animals, produced from the emotion of ignorance, will also meet them. At that time, to show him again, one should call the dead person by name and say these words: ⸱⸱

"O child of noble family, listen without distraction. On the seventh day a pure, many colored light will shine in your unconscious mind, and the vidyādharas will come from the Pure Realm of Space to invite you. In the center of a maṇḍala filled with rainbow light, he who is called the Unsurpassable Fully Developed Vidyādhara, Lotus Lord of Dance, will appear, his body bright with the five colors, embracing his consort the Red Ḍākinī, dancing with a crescent knife and a skull full of blood, gesturing and gazing at the sky. ⸱⸱

"From the east of the maṇḍala he who is called the Vidyādhara Established in the

Stages[11] will appear, white in color, with a radiant smiling face, embracing his consort the White Ḍākinī, dancing with a crescent knife and a skull full of blood, gesturing and gazing at the sky. ⁖

"From the south of the maṇḍala he who is called the Lord of Life Vidyādhara will appear, yellow in color, with beautiful form, embracing his consort the Yellow Ḍākinī, dancing with a crescent knife and a skull full of blood, gesturing and gazing at the sky. ⁖

"From the west of the maṇḍala he who is called the Great Symbol Vidyādhara will appear, red in color, with a radiant smiling face, embracing his consort the Red Ḍākinī, dancing with a crescent knife and a skull full of blood, gesturing and gazing at the sky. ⁖

"From the north of the maṇḍala he who is called the Spontaneously Arisen Vidyādhara will appear, green in color, his expression both angry and smiling, embracing his consort the Green Ḍākinī, dancing with a crescent knife and a skull full of blood, gesturing and gazing at the sky.°

"Beyond those vidyādharas will appear countless crowds of ḍākinīs: ḍākinīs of the eight charnel-grounds, ḍākinīs of the four families, ḍākinīs of the three worlds, ḍākinīs of the ten directions, ḍākinīs of the twenty-four places of pilgrimage; male and female warriors and servants, and all the male and female protectors of dharma, wearing the six bone-ornaments, with drums, thigh-bone trumpets, skull-drums, banners made from the skins of youths, canopies made from human skin, ribbons of human skin and incense made from human flesh, with countless different kinds of musical instruments, filling all the regions of the universe so that they rock and tremble and shake, making all the instruments vibrate with music so as to split one's head, dancing various dances, they will come to invite those who have kept the samaya practice and to punish those who have let it degenerate.⸪

"O child of noble family, in the realm of the unconscious, the pure innate wisdom, shining with the five colored lights like colored threads twisted together, flashing, vibrating, shimmering, luminous and clear, sharp and terrifying, will come from the hearts of the five vidyādhara lords and pierce your heart so that the eye cannot bear it. At the same time the soft green light of the animals will also shine together with the wisdom light. At that time, under the influence of confusion caused by unconscious tendencies, you will be afraid and escape from the five-colored light, but you will be attracted to the soft light of the animals. At that moment do not be afraid of the bright, sharp, five-colored light; do not fear it, but recognize it as wisdom. ⸪

"From within the light all the spontaneous sounds of the dharma will come like the roar of a thousand thunder-claps. It rolls and thunders and resounds with war-cries and the penetrating sound of wrathful mantras. Do not be afraid of it, do not escape, do not fear. Recognize it as the play of your mind, your own projection. Do not be attracted to the soft green light of the animals, do not yearn for it; if you are attracted to it you will fall into the animal realm of ignorance and experience the extreme suffering of stupidity, dumbness and slavery, from which there is no escape; so do not be attracted to it. Feel longing for the clear, bright light of the five colors, and concentrate one-pointedly on the blessed vidyādharas, the divine teachers, thinking, 'These vidyādharas with the warriors and ḍākinīs have come

to invite me to the Pure Realm of Space.
Please all give thought to sentient beings
like me who have not gathered merit and
have not been caught, although until today
the light-rays of compassion of so many
deities of the five families of buddhas of
past, present and future reached out. Alas
for one like me! Now all you vidyādharas,
do not let me go any lower than this, but
grasp me with your hooks of compassion
and pull me up quickly to the Pure Realm
of Space.'⁖

"With intense one-pointed concentration say this inspiration-prayer:⁖

May the divine vidyādharas think of me
and with great love lead me on the path.
When through intense tendencies
    I wander in saṃsāra,
on the luminous light-path of
    the innate wisdom,
may vidyādharas and warriors
    go before me,

their consorts the ḍākinīs behind me;
help me to cross the bardo's dangerous
pathway
and bring me to the Pure Realm of Space." ❖

By saying this inspiration-prayer with deep devotion, he will dissolve into rainbow light in the heart of the divine vidyā-dharas, and be born in the Pure Realm of Space, there is no doubt. All the types of spiritual friends, too, recognize as a result of this and are all liberated; even those with bad unconscious tendencies are certainly liberated here. ❖

The end of the first part of
"The Great Liberation through Hearing":
showing the luminosity during the bardo
of the moment before death, and
showing during the peaceful
bardo of the dharmatā. ❖

iti ❖ samaya ❖ rgya rgya rgya ❖

Now it will be taught how the bardo of the wrathful deities appears.⸫

Up to now there have been seven stages in the dangerous pathway of the bardo of the peaceful deities, and by being shown at each of the stages, even if he has not recognized at one he will have at another, and boundless attainments of liberation occur. But although many are liberated like this, sentient beings are great in number, bad karma is very strong, the veils of error are heavy and thick, the unconscious tendencies last for a long time, and this cycle of confusion and ignorance neither wears out nor increases, so there are many who are not liberated but wander downwards, although they have been shown accurately in this way.⸫

So then, after the meeting by the peaceful deities and vidyādharas and ḍākinīs is over, the fifty-eight blazing, blood-drinking wrathful deities will appear, transformed from the previous peaceful deities. But now they are not like they were before; this is the bardo of the wrathful deities, so one is overpowered by intense fear and it becomes more difficult to recognize. The mind has no self-control and feels faint and dizzy, but if there is a little recognition liberation is easy, because with the arising of overwhelming fear the mind has no time to be distracted, and so it concentrates one-pointedly. ⁑

If one does not meet with this kind of teaching now, even an ocean of learning will be no use. At this point even teachers who observe the monastic rule and great philosophers are confused and do not recognize, so they go on wandering in samsāra. It is even more so for ordinary people; escaping from the intense fear they fall into the lower realms and suffer misery. But a tantric yogin, even if he is the lowest of the low, will recognize the blood-drinking deities as yidams as soon as he sees them, like meeting old friends, so he

will trust them, and merging inseparably
with them become a buddha. The secret is
that in the human world he visualized the
forms of these blood-drinking deities and
worshipped them, and even if he only
looked at their images drawn in pictures
or three-dimensional figures and so on, he
will recognize the forms appearing here
and attain liberation. ⁙

But however much effort the philosophers and teachers who observe the rule
made in religious practice, and however
clever they were at preaching the scriptures in the human world, when they die
there will not be any signs such as jewell-
like relics,[12] rainbows, and so on. While
they were alive they cast abuse at the tantras and could not accommodate them in
their minds; they did not know the tantric
deities, therefore they cannot recognize
them when they appear in the bardo either. Suddenly seeing something they have
never seen before, they think of it as an

enemy and feel aggression towards it, and as a result they go to the lower realms. That is the reason why, however good those philosophers and observers of the rule were, since they did not practice the tantras, signs such as various kinds of jewel-like relics and rainbows do not occur among them. ⁚

A follower of tantra, even if he is the lowest of the low, however coarsely he behaved in this world and however uncultured and unrefined he was, even if he was unable to practice the tantric teachings, just because he had faith in the tantras and did not have any doubt or disbelief will attain liberation at this point; so although his behavior was unconventional in the human world, when he dies at least one sign such as jewel-like relics or rainbows will appear. This is because this tantric teaching has very great power. ⁚

Tantric yogins who are above average, who have meditated on the generation and perfection stages and practiced recitation of heart-mantras and so on, need not wander so far down in the bardo of dharmatā, but as soon as they stop breathing, the vidyādharas, warriors and ḍākinīs will invite them to the Pure Realm of Space. As a sign of this the sky clears and they dissolve into rainbow light, and rain of flowers, fragrance of incense, sounds of musical instruments in the air, light-rays, jewel-like relics and so on appear: these are the signs. ⸖

Therefore those philosophers and observers of the rule, followers of tantra who have let their samaya practice degenerate, and all ordinary people, have no means except this "Great Liberation through Hearing." Meditators who have practiced the Great Symbol and Great Completion[13] meditations and so on will recognize the luminosity in the bardo of the moment before death and reach the dharmakāya, so it is absolutely unnecessary to read this "Great Liberation through Hearing." ⸖

If they recognize the luminosity during the bardo of the moment before death they will reach the dharmakāya. If they recognize during the bardo of dharmatā when the peaceful and wrathful deities appear they will reach the saṃbhogakāya. If they recognize during the bardo of becoming they will reach the nirmāṇakāya and be born in a better situation where they will meet with this teaching; and since the results of actions continue in the next life, that is why this "Great Liberation through Hearing" is a teaching which enlightens without meditation, a teaching which liberates just by being heard, a teaching which leads great sinners on the secret path, a teaching which severs ignorance in one moment, a profound teaching which gives perfect instantaneous enlightenment, so that sentient beings whom it has reached cannot possibly go to lower existences. Both it and the "Liberation through Wearing"[14] should be read aloud, for the two combined are like a golden maṇḍala inlaid with turquoise.⸪

Now that the great necessity of the "Liberation through Hearing" has been taught in this way, it will be shown how the bardo of the wrathful deities appears. Calling the dead person three times by name, one should say these words:⸪

"O child of noble family, listen without distraction. Although the bardo of the peaceful deities has already appeared, you did not recognize, so you have wandered further on to here. Now on the eighth day the blood-drinking wrathful deities will appear. Recognize them without being distracted.⸪

"O child of noble family, he who is called Glorious Great Buddha-Heruka[15] will emerge from within your own brain and appear before you actually and clearly: his body is wine-colored, with three heads, six arms, and four legs spread wide apart; the right face is white, the left one red, and the center one wine-colored; his body blazes like a mass of light, his nine eyes gaze into yours with a wrathful expression, his eyebrows are like flashes of lightning, his teeth gleam like copper; he laughs aloud with shouts of "a-la-la!" and "ha-ha!" and sends out loud whistling noises of "shoo-oo!" His red-gold hair flies upwards blazing, his heads are crowned with dried skulls and the sun and moon, his body is garlanded with black serpents and fresh skulls; his six hands hold a wheel in the first hand on the right, an axe in the middle, and a sword in the last, a bell in the first on the left, a plough-share in the middle, and a skull-cup in the last; his consort Buddha-Krodhīśvarī embraces his body, with her right hand clasped around his neck and her left hand holding a skull full of blood to his mouth; he sends out loud palatal sounds and roaring sounds like thunder; flames of wisdom shoot out from between the blazing vajra hairs on his body; he stands on a throne supported by garuḍas, with one pair of legs bent and the other stretched out. ፨

"Do not be afraid of him, do not be terrified, do not be bewildered. Recognize him as the form of your own mind. He is your yidam, so do not be afraid. He is really Blessed Vairocana with his consort, so do not fear. Recognition and liberation are simultaneous." ፨

When this is said, he will recognize the yidam, and merging inseparably with it become a buddha in the saṃbhogakāya. ፨

But if he is afraid of it and escapes, and so does not recognize, then on the ninth day the blood-drinking manifestation of the Vajra family will come to invite him, so to show him again one should call the dead person by name and say these words: ፨

"O child of noble family, listen without distraction. On the ninth day the blood-drinking manifestation of the Vajra family, called Blessed Vajra-Heruka, will emerge from the eastern quarter of your brain and appear before you: his body is dark blue in color, with three heads, six arms, and four legs spread wide apart; the right face is white, the left one red, and the center one blue; his six hands hold a vajra in the first on the right, a skull-cup in the middle, and an axe in the last, a bell in the first on the left, a skull-cup in the middle, and a plough-share in the last; his consort Vajra-Krodhīśvarī embraces his body, with her right hand clasped around his neck and her left hand holding a skull full of blood to his mouth. ፨

"Do not be afraid of him, do not be terrified, do not be bewildered. Recognize him as the form of your own mind. He is your yidam, so do not be afraid. He is really Blessed Vajrasattva with his consort, so have devotion. Recognition and liberation are simultaneous." ፨

When this is said, he will recognize the

yidam, and merging inseparably with it become a buddha in the saṃbhogakāya.⁝

But if those whose karmic darkness is great are afraid of it and escape, and so do not recognize, then on the tenth day the blood-drinking manifestation of the Ratna family will come to invite them. So, to show him again, one should call the dead person by name and say these words:⁝

"O child of noble family, listen without distraction. On the tenth day the blood-drinking manifestation of the Ratna family, called Blessed Ratna-Heruka, will appear before you from the southern quarter of your brain: his body is dark yellow in color, with three heads, six arms, and four legs spread wide apart; the right face is white, the left one red, and the center one blazing dark yellow; his six hands hold a jewel in the first on the right, a trident bearing three human heads in the middle, and a club in the last, a bell in the first on the left, a skull-cup in the middle, and a trident in the last; his consort Ratna-Krodhīśvarī embraces his body, with her right hand clasped around his neck and her left hand holding a skull full of blood to his mouth.⁘

"Do not be afraid of him, do not be terrified, do not be bewildered. Recognize him as the form of your own mind. He is your yidam, so do not be afraid. He is really Blessed Ratnasambhava with his consort, so feel longing. Recognition and liberation are simultaneous."⁘

When this is said, he will recognize the yidam, and merging inseparably with it become a buddha.⁘

But if, even after being shown like this, he is pulled back by evil unconscious tendencies and is afraid and escapes, and so does not recognize the yidam, if even when he sees Yamāntaka he does not recognize him, then on the eleventh day the blood-drinking manifestation of the Padma family will come to invite him. So, to show him again, one should call the dead person by name and say these words: :

"O child of noble family, listen without distraction. On the eleventh day the blood-drinking manifestation of the Padma family, called Blessed Padma-Heruka, will emerge from the western quarter of your brain and appear before you clearly in union with his consort. His body is dark red in color, with three heads, six arms, and four legs spread wide apart; the right face is white, the left one blue, and the center one dark red; his six hands hold a lotus in the first on the right, a trident bearing three human heads in the middle, and a rod in the last, a bell in the first on the left, a skull-cup filled with blood in the middle, and a small drum in the last; his consort Padma-Krodhīśvarī embraces his body, with her right hand clasped around his neck and her left hand holding a skull full of blood to his mouth. :

"Do not be afraid of him, do not be

terrified, do not be bewildered. Be joyful, and recognize him as the form of your own mind. He is your yidam, so do not be afraid, do not be terrified. He is really Blessed Amitābha with his consort, so feel longing. Recognition and liberation are simultaneous." ⸙

When this is said, he will recognize it to be the yidam, and merging inseparably with it become a buddha. ⸙

But if, even after being shown like this, he is pulled back by evil unconscious tendencies and is afraid and escapes, and so cannot recognize the yidam, then on the twelfth day the blood-drinking manifestation of the Karma family will come, with the gaurīs, piśācīs and yoginīs,[16] to invite him. If he does not recognize he will be afraid, so to show him again one should call the dead person by name and say these words: ⸙

"O child of noble family, listen without

distraction. When the twelfth day has come, the blood-drinking manifestation of the Karma family, called Blessed Karma-Heruka, will emerge from the northern quarter of your brain and appear before you clearly in union with his consort; his body is dark green in color, with three heads, six arms, and four legs spread wide apart; the right face is white, the left one red, and the center one majestic dark green; his six hands hold a sword in the first on the right, a trident bearing three human heads in the middle, and a rod in the last, a bell in the first on the left, a skull-cup in the middle, and a plough-share in the last; his consort Karma-Krodhīśvarī embraces his body, with her right hand clasped around his neck and her left hand holding a skull full of blood to his mouth. ⁝

"Do not be afraid of him, do not be terrified, do not be bewildered. Recognize him as the form of your own mind. He is your yidam, so do not be afraid. He is really Blessed Amoghasiddhi with his consort, so feel intense devotion. Recognition and liberation are simultaneous."⫶

When this is said, he will recognize the yidam, and merging inseparably with it become a buddha.⫶

Through the instruction of his guru he will recognize them as his own projections, the play of the mind, and he will be liberated. It is just like seeing a stuffed lion, for instance: he feels very frightened if he does not know that it is really only a stuffed lion, but if someone shows him what it is he is astonished and no longer afraid. So here too he feels terrified and bewildered when the blood-drinking deities appear with their huge bodies and thick limbs, filling the whole of space, but as soon as he is shown he recognizes them as his own projections or as yidams; the luminosity on which he has meditated before and the self-existing luminosity which arises later, mother and son, merge together, and, like meeting someone he used to know very well, the self-liberating luminosity of his own mind spontaneously arises before him, and he is self-liberated.⸪

If he does not receive this showing, even a good person can turn back from here and wander in saṃsāra. Then the eight wrathful gaurīs and the piśācīs with various heads will emerge from within his own brain and appear before him, so to show him again one should call the dead person by name and say these words:⸪

"O child of noble family, listen without distraction. The eight gaurīs will emerge from within your own brain and appear before you. Do not be afraid of them.⸪

"From the eastern quarter of your brain white Gaurī will appear to you, holding a corpse as a club in her right hand and a skull-cup filled with blood in her left hand. Do not be afraid. From the south yellow Caurī, shooting an arrow from a bow; from the west red Pramohā, holding a sea-monster banner; from the north black Vetālī, holding a vajra and a skull-cup filled with blood; from the south-east orange Pukkasī, holding entrails in her right hand and eating them with her left; from the south-west dark green Ghasmarī, drinking from a skull-cup filled with blood, which she holds in her left hand and stirs with a vajra with her right hand; from the north-west pale yellow Caṇḍālī, tearing a head and body apart, holding the heart in her right hand and eating the body with her left; from the north-east dark blue Śmaśānī, tearing a head and body apart, and eating; these eight gaurīs of the directions, surrounding the five blood-drinking herukas, will emerge from within your own brain and appear before you. Do not be afraid of them.⁘

"O child of noble family, listen without distraction. After them in turn the eight piśācīs of the holy places will emerge and appear before you.⁘

"From the east Siṅhamukhā, wine-colored, lion-headed, with her two hands crossed on her breast, holding a corpse in her mouth and tossing her mane; from the south Vyāghrīmukhā, red, tiger-headed, with her two arms crossed pointing downwards, her eyes staring and her teeth snarling; from the west Śṛgālamukhā, black, fox-headed, holding a razor in her right hand and entrails in her left, eating them and licking the blood; from the north Śvānamukhā, dark blue, wolf-headed, carrying a corpse to her mouth with both hands, her eyes staring; from the south-east Gṛdhramukhā, pale yellow, vulture-headed, carrying a large human corpse over her shoulder and holding a skeleton in her hand; from the south-west Kaṅkamukhā, dark red, hawk-headed, carrying a large flayed skin over her shoulder; from the north-west Kākamukhā, black, raven-headed, holding a skull-cup in her left hand and a sword in her right, and eating a heart and lungs; from the north-east Ulumukhā, dark blue, owl-headed, holding a vajra in her right hand and a sword in her left, and eating: these eight piśācīs of the holy places, surrounding the five blood-drinking herukas, will emerge from within your own brain and appear before you. Do not be afraid of them. Recognize whatever appears as the play of the mind, your own projections. ⸱

"O child of noble family, the four goddesses of the gates will also emerge from within your brain and appear before you, so recognize them. ⸱

"From the eastern quarter of your

brain, Aṅkuśā, white, tiger-headed, holding a goad and a skull-cup filled with blood, will emerge and appear before you; from the south Pāśā, yellow, sow-headed, holding a noose; from the west Śṛṅkhalā, red, lion-headed, holding an iron chain; and from the north Ghaṇṭā, green, serpent-headed, holding a bell: these four goddesses of the gates will emerge from within your own brain and appear before you. Recognize them as yidams.⁝

"O child of noble family, after the thirty wrathful herukas, the twenty-eight yoginīs will emerge in turn from within your brain and appear before you, with various heads and bearing various symbols. Do not be afraid of them, but recognize whatever appears as the play of the mind, your own projections. At this moment of reaching the crucial point, remember the instructions of your guru.⁝

"O child of noble family, from the east,

the six yoginīs of the east will emerge from within your brain and appear before you: Rākṣasī, Demoness, wine-colored, with the head of a yak, holding a vajra in her hand; Brāhmī, orange, serpent-headed, holding a lotus in her hand; Mahādevī, Great Goddess, dark green, leopard-headed, holding a trident in her hand; Lobhā, Greedy, blue, mongoose-headed, holding a wheel in her hand; Kumārī, Virgin, red, with the head of a yellow bear, holding a short spear in her hand; and Indrāṇī, white, with the head of a brown bear, holding a noose of entrails in her hand. Do not be afraid of them. ⸭

"O child of noble family, from the south the six yoginīs of the south will emerge from within your brain and appear before you: Vajrā, yellow, with the head of a pig, holding a razor in her hand; Śānti, Peace, red, with the head of a sea-monster, holding a vase in her hand; Amṛtā, Nectar of Immortality, red, scorpion-headed, holding a lotus in her hand; Candrā, Moon, white, hawk-headed, holding a vajra in her hand; Daṇḍā, Club, dark green, fox-headed, holding a club in her hand; and Rākṣasī, Demoness, dark yellow, tiger-headed, holding a skull full of blood in her hand. Do not be afraid of them. ⁑

"O child of noble family, from the west the six yoginīs of the west will emerge from within your brain and appear before you: Bhakṣiṇī, Eater, dark green, vulture-headed, holding a club in her hand; Rati, Pleasure, red, horse-headed, holding a large corpse's trunk in her hand; Mahā-balā, Great Strength, white, garuḍa-headed, holding a club in her hand; Rāk-ṣasī, Demoness, red, dog-headed, cutting with a vajra-razor in her hand; Kāmā, De-sire, red, with the head of a hoopoe, shooting an arrow from a bow in her hand; and Vasurakṣā, Protectress of Wealth, dark green, with the head of a deer, holding a vase in her hand. Do not be afraid of them. ⁜

"O child of noble family, from the north the six yoginīs of the north will emerge from within your brain and appear before you: Vāyudevī, Wind-Goddess, blue, wolf-headed, waving a flag in her hand; Nārī, Woman, red, buffalo-headed, holding a stake in her hand; Vārāhī, Sow, black, with the head of a sow, holding a noose of teeth in her hand; Vajrā, red, with the head of a crow, holding a child's skin in her hand; Mahāhastinī, Elephant, dark green, elephant-headed, holding a large corpse in her hand and drinking its blood; and Varuṇadevī, Water-Goddess, blue, serpent-headed, holding a noose of snakes in her hand. Do not be afraid of them. ⁜

"O child of noble family, the four yoginīs of the gates will emerge from within your brain and appear before you: from the east, white Vajrā, cuckoo-headed, holding an iron hook in her hand; from the south, yellow Vajrā, goat-headed, holding a noose in her hand; from the west, red Vajrā, lion-headed, holding an iron chain in her hand; and from the north, dark green Vajrā, serpent-headed, holding a bell in her hand: these four yoginīs of the gates will emerge from within your brain and appear before you. ⁘

"These twenty-eight yoginīs arise spontaneously from the play of the self-existing form of the wrathful herukas, so recognize them. ⁘

"O child of noble family, the dharmakāya appears as the peaceful deities out of part of the emptiness; recognize it. The saṃbhogakāya appears as the wrathful deities out of part of the luminosity, so recognize it. If at this time when the fifty-eight blood-drinking deities emerge from within your brain and appear before you,

you know that whatever appears has arisen out of your own radiant insight, you will immediately become a buddha inseparable from the blood-drinking deities. ⸭

"O child of noble family, if you do not recognize in this way, you will be afraid of them and escape, and so go on to more suffering. If you do not recognize in this way, you will see all the blood-drinking deities as Lords of Death, and you will fear them. You will feel terrified and bewildered and faint. Your own projections will turn into demons and you will wander in saṃsāra. But if you are neither attracted nor afraid you will not wander in saṃsāra. ⸭

"O child of noble family, the largest bodies of these peaceful and wrathful deities are like the whole sky, the medium ones are like Mount Meru, and the smallest ones are like eighteen of our bodies one on top of the other, so do not be afraid of them. All phenomena appear as lights and images; by recognizing all these appearances as the natural radiance of your own mind, your own radiance will merge inseparably with the lights and images, and you will become a buddha. O child, whatever you see, however terrifying it is, recognize it as your own projection; recognize it as the luminosity, the natural radiance of your own mind. If you recognize in this way, you will become a buddha at that very moment, there is no doubt. What is called perfect instantaneous enlightenment will arise on the spot. Remember!⸭

"O child of noble family, if you do not recognize now and are still afraid, all the peaceful deities will appear in the form of Mahākāla, and all the wrathful deities will appear in the form of the Dharma King, the Lord of Death, and you will wander in saṃsāra with all your projections turned into demons.⸭

"O child of noble family, if you do not recognize your own projections, even though you have practiced dharma for an eon and are learned in all the sūtras and tantras, you will not become a buddha. But if you recognize your projections, with one secret and one word you will become a buddha.÷

"If you do not recognize your projections, they will appear in the form of the Dharma King, the Lord of Death, in the bardo of dharmatā as soon as you are dead. The largest bodies of the Lords of Death fill the whole sky and the medium ones are like Mount Meru; they will come filling the whole universe. With teeth biting the lower lip, glassy-eyed, their hair tied on top of their heads, with huge bellies and thin necks, holding the records of karma in their hands, shouting 'Strike!' and 'Kill!,' licking up brains, tearing heads from bodies, pulling out internal organs: in this way they will come, filling the whole universe. ⸭

"O child of noble family, when projections appear like this do not be afraid. You have a mental body of unconscious tendencies, so even if you are killed and cut into pieces you cannot die. You are really the natural form of emptiness, so there is no need to fear. The Lords of Death too arise out of your own radiant mind, they have no solid substance. Emptiness cannot be harmed by emptiness. Be certain that the external peaceful and wrathful deities, the blood-drinking herukas, the animal-headed deities, the rainbow light, the terrifying forms of the Lords of Death and so on have no substantiality, they only arise out of the spontaneous play of your mind. If you understand this, all fear is naturally liberated, and merging inseparably you will become a buddha. If you recognize in this way, they are your yidams. ⸭

"Think with intense longing, 'They have come to invite me in the dangerous pathway of the bardo; I take refuge in them.' Remember the Three Jewels. Remember your own yidam; call his name and supplicate him with these words: 'I am wandering in the bardo, so be my rescuer, seize me with compassion, O precious yidam.' Call your guru's name and supplicate him: 'I am wandering in the bardo, so be my rescuer, with your compassion do not abandon me.' Supplicate the blood-drinking deities with longing, and say this inspiration-prayer: ॰

When through strong unconscious
    tendencies I wander in saṃsāra,
in the luminosity of abandoning all fear,
may the Blessed Ones, peaceful and
    wrathful, go before me,
the wrathful goddesses, Queens of Space,
    behind me;

help me to cross the bardo's dangerous
   pathway
and bring me to the perfect buddha state.
When parted from beloved friends,
   wandering alone,
my own projections' empty forms appear,
may the buddhas send out the power
   of their compassion
so that the bardo's terrors do not come.
When the five luminous lights of wisdom
   shine,
fearlessly may I recognize myself;
when the forms of the peaceful and
   wrathful ones appear,
fearless and confident may I recognize
   the bardo.
When I suffer through the power of
   evil karma,
may my yidam clear away all suffering;
when the sound of dharmatā roars
   like a thousand thunders,
may it all become the sound of
   the six syllables.[17]

*When I follow my karma, without
    a refuge,
may the Lord of Great Compassion
    be my refuge;
when I suffer the karma of unconscious
    tendencies,
may the samādhi of bliss and luminosity
    arise.
May the five elements not rise up
    as enemies,
may I see the realms of
    the five buddhas.* ÷

"Say this inspiration-prayer with deep
devotion. All fears will disappear and you
will certainly become a buddha in the
sambhogakāya, so it is very important; do
not be distracted." ÷

These words should be repeated three
or up to seven times. However great the
sins and however bad the remaining karma
may be, it is impossible not to be liberated.
But if, whatever is done for them, they do

not recognize, then they have to wander in the third bardo, the bardo of becoming, so its showing will be taught in detail below.⸙

Most people, whether they were much or little adept in meditation, are very confused by fear during the bardo of the moment before death, and so they have no means except this "Liberation through Hearing." To those who have meditated a lot, the bardo of dharmatā comes suddenly when their mind and body separate. Those who have recognized their own mind and become experienced while they were alive are very strong when the luminosity appears during the bardo of the moment before death, therefore practice during life is most important. And those who, while they were alive, have meditated on the generation and perfection stages of the tantric deities, are very strong when the peaceful and wrathful visions appear during the bardo of dharmatā. Therefore it is extremely important to train the mind thoroughly in this "Liberation through Hearing in the Bardo," especially during one's life. ⸭

It should be grasped, it should be perfected, it should be read aloud, it should be memorized properly, it should be practiced three times a day without fail, the meaning of its words should be made completely clear in the mind, its words and meaning should not be forgotten even if a hundred murderers were to appear and chase one. Since this is called "The Great Liberation through Hearing," even people who have committed the five deadly sins will certainly be liberated if they only hear it; therefore it should be read aloud among great crowds, and spread afar. ⸭

Even if it has been heard like this only once and the meaning not understood, in the bardo state the mind becomes nine times more clear, so then it will be remembered with not even a single word forgotten. Therefore it should be told to all during their life, it should be read at the bedside of all the sick, it should be read beside the bodies of all the dead, it should be spread far and wide. ⁝

To meet with it is great good fortune; it is hard to meet with except for those who have cleared away their darkness and gathered merit. If one hears it, one is liberated simply by not disbelieving, therefore it should be greatly cherished; it draws out the essence of all dharma. ⁝

The end of the showing of the bardo of dharmatā, called "The Great Liberation through Hearing," the bardo teaching which liberates just by being heard and seen. ⁝

sarvamaṅgalam ⁝

Respectful homage to the deities:
gurus, yidams and ḍākinīs;
may they cause liberation in the bardo.
In "The Great Liberation through
*   Hearing"*
the bardo of dharmatā has been taught
*   above,*
now comes the reminder of the bardo
*   of becoming. ⁙*

Although the bardo of dharmatā has been shown many times before this, apart from those who were adept in meditation on dharma and have good karmic results, because of fear and bad karma recognition is difficult for those who were not adept or who were very wicked. So from about the tenth day onwards they should be reminded again in these words: ⁙

"O child of noble family, listen well and understand. Hell-beings, gods and the bardo body are born spontaneously. When the peaceful and wrathful deities appeared in the bardo of dharmatā you did not recognize them, so you fainted with fear after five and a half days; but when you recovered your consciousness grew clear, and a body like your former one rose up. It is said in the tantra: ❖

> With the former and future material body
>   of the bardo of becoming,
> complete with all the senses, wandering
>   without obstruction,
> possessing the power of miracles resulting
>   from karma,
> seen by the pure eyes of gods with
>   the same nature. ❖

"Here 'former' means that you have a body like your former one of flesh and blood because of your memories of it, but it is also radiant and has some marks like a body of the golden age. This is the experience of a mental body, so it is called the mental body of the bardo experience. At this time, if you are going to be born as a god, you will experience the realm of the gods, and whatever you are going to be born as, jealous god, human, animal, hungry ghost or hell-being, you will have that experience. Therefore 'former' means thinking for up to four and a half days that you have a material body of memories of your former one, and 'future' means that after that you will have experiences of wherever you are going to be born later; so they say 'former and future.'⸫

"Whatever projections arise at this time, do not follow them or be attracted to them or yearn for them. If you are attracted to them or yearn for them you will wander in the six realms and suffer misery.⸫

"Although the projections of the bardo of dharmatā appeared until yesterday, you did not recognize them, so you had to

wander here. Now, if you are able to meditate undistractedly, rest in the pure, naked mind, luminosity-emptiness, which
your guru has shown you, relaxed in a
state of non-grasping and non-action. You
will attain liberation and not enter a
womb.⸪

"If you cannot recognize, visualize your
yidam or your guru above your head and
feel intense devotion very strongly. This is
very important. Again and again, do not be
distracted."⸪

So one should say. If he recognizes this
he will be liberated and not wander in the
six realms. But under the influence of bad
karma it is difficult to recognize, so one
should say these words:⸪

"O child of noble family, listen with undistracted mind. 'Complete with all the
senses' means that even if you were blind,
deaf, lame and so on when you were alive,
now in the bardo state your eyes see

forms, your ears hear sounds, and all your senses are clear and faultless; so it is said, 'complete with all the senses.' This is a sign that you have died and are wandering in the bardo state, so recognize, remember the instruction. ⦂

"O child of noble family, 'without obstruction' means that as you are a mental body and your mind is separated from its support, you have no material body, so now you can pass back and forth even through Mount Meru, the king of mountains, or anywhere except your mother's womb and the vajra seat.[18] This is a sign that you are wandering in the bardo of becoming, so remember your guru's teaching and supplicate the Lord of Great Compassion. ⦂

"O child of noble family, 'possessing the power of miracles resulting from karma' means that now you have miraculous powers resulting from the force of karma in accordance with your actions, not those which come from meditation or virtues. You can circle the four continents and Mount Meru in an instant, and arrive anywhere you want instantaneously as soon as you think of it, or in the time it takes a man to stretch out and draw back his hand. But these various powers are unsuitable; do not think about them. Now you have the ability to display them without hindrance, you can perform everything you think of and there is no action you cannot do, so recognize, and supplicate your guru. ⸫

"O child of noble family, 'seen by the pure eyes of gods with the same nature' means that those who are going to be born with the same nature will see one another in the bardo state, so those who are going to be born as gods see each other. In the same way, whichever of the six realms they are going to be born in, those of the same

nature will see each other. Do not yearn
for them, but meditate on the Lord of
Great Compassion. 'Seen by the pure eyes
of gods' also means seen by the pure divine
eye of meditators in real samādhi, and not
only that which comes from the merit of
the gods. But they do not always see; if
they concentrate on seeing they will see,
but if not, or if their meditation is disturbed, they do not see. ॰

"O child of noble family, with a body
like this you will see your home and family
as though you were meeting them in a
dream, but although you speak to them
you will get no reply; and you will see
your relatives and family weeping, so you
will think, 'I am dead, what shall I do?' and
you will feel intense pain like the pain of a
fish rolling in hot sand. But now suffering
is no use. If you have a guru, supplicate
him, or supplicate the yidam, the Lord of
Great Compassion. Even though you are

attached to your relatives it is no use, so do not be attached. Supplicate the Lord of Great Compassion, and there will be no suffering or fear.⁑

"O child of noble family, blown by the moving wind of karma, your mind, without support, helplessly rides the horse of wind like a feather, swaying and swinging. You will say to the mourners, 'I am here, do not weep,' but they will not perceive you, so you will think, 'I have died,' and now you will feel great pain. Do not suffer like that. All the time there will be a grey haze like the grey light of an autumn dawn, neither day nor night. This kind of bardo state will last for one, two, three, four, five, six or seven weeks, up to forty-nine days. It is said that the suffering in the bardo of becoming generally lasts for twenty-one days, but this is not quite certain because of the influence of karma.⁑

"O child of noble family, at this time

the great tornado of karma, terrifying, unbearable, whirling fiercely, will drive you
from behind. Do not be afraid of it; it is
your own confused projection. Dense
darkness, terrifying and unbearable, will
go before you, with terrible cries of
'Strike!' and 'Kill!' Do not be afraid of
them. In the case of others who have done
great evil, many flesh-eating demons will
appear as a result of their karma, bearing
various weapons, yelling war cries, shouting 'Kill! Strike!,' and so on. You will feel
that you are being chased by various terrifying wild animals and pursued by a great
army in snow, rain, storms and darkness.
There will be sounds of mountains crum-
bling, of lakes flooding, of fire spreading,
and of fierce winds springing up. In fear
you will escape wherever you can, but you
will be cut off by three precipices in front
of you, white, red and black, deep and

dreadful, and you will be on the point of falling down them.⸭

"O child of noble family, they are not really precipices, they are aggression, passion and ignorance. Recognize this now to be the bardo of becoming, and call the name of the Lord of Great Compassion: 'O Lord of Great Compassion, my guru, the Three Jewels, do not let me, (name), fall into hell.' Supplicate fervently like this; do not forget.⸭

"In the case of others who have gathered merit and were virtuous and practiced dharma sincerely, all kinds of perfect enjoyment will invite them, and they will experience all kinds of perfect bliss and happiness. In the case of those who were indifferent and ignorant, who did neither good nor evil, they will not experience pleasure or pain, but only ignorance and indifference will appear. Whatever arises like this, O child of noble family, whatever pleasures and objects of desire, do not be attracted to them or yearn for them. Offer them to the guru and the Three Jewels. Give up attachment and longing in your heart. And if the experience of indifference arises without either pleasure or pain, rest your mind in the Great Symbol state of undistracted non-meditation. This is very important. :

"O child of noble family, at this time bridges, shrines and monasteries, huts, stūpas and so on will shelter you for a moment, but you will not stay there for long. Since your mind is separated from your body you cannot settle down, you feel angry and cold, and consciousness becomes airy, speeding, swaying and impermanent. Then you will think, 'Alas, I am dead! What shall I do now?' and thinking this your heart will suddenly grow empty and cold, and you will feel intense and boundless pain. Since you must move on without settling in any one place, do not occupy yourself with all kinds of thoughts, but rest your mind in its basic state.⸫

"The time comes when you have no food except that which has been dedicated for you to eat, and there is no certainty of friends. These are signs of the mental body wandering in the bardo of becoming. At this moment pleasure and pain are determined by your karma. You will see your homeland, friends and relatives, and your own corpse, and you will think, 'Now I am dead, so what should I do?' The mental body will be in extreme pain, so you will think, 'Now why not find a body?' and you will experience going everywhere to look for a body. Even if you enter your own corpse up to nine times, winter will have frozen it or summer made it rot, or else your relatives will have burned it or buried it in a grave or given it to the birds and wild animals, for a long time has passed in the bardo of dharmatā, so you will find nowhere to enter; you will be in great despair, and have the feeling of being squeezed in between all the rocks and stones. Suffering like this is the bardo of becoming, even if you look for a body there is nothing but suffering, so cut off your yearning for a body and rest in the state of non-action, undistracted."⸭

By being shown in this way, liberation from the bardo is attained. But if, in spite of being shown like this, it is impossible to recognize because of the power of bad karma, one should call the dead person by name and say these words:⸭

"O child of noble family, (name), listen. It is your own karma, that you are suffering like this, so you cannot blame anyone else. It is your own karma, so now supplicate the Three Jewels fervently, they will protect you. If you do not supplicate like this, and do not know the Great Symbol meditation, and do not meditate on your yidam, then the good conscience within you will collect all your good actions and count out white pebbles, and the bad conscience within you will collect all your evil actions and count out black pebbles. At this time you will be very frightened and terrified, and you will tremble and lie, saying, 'I have not sinned.' Then the Lord of Death will say, 'I will look in the mirror of karma,' and when he looks in the mirror all your sins and virtues will suddenly appear in it clearly and distinctly, so although you have lied it is no use. Then the Lord of Death will drag you by a rope tied round your neck, and cut off your head, tear out your heart, pull out your entrails, lick your brains, drink your blood, eat your flesh and gnaw your bones; but you cannot die, so even though your body is cut into pieces you will recover.⁖

"Being cut again and again causes extreme pain, so do not be afraid when the white pebbles are being counted, do not lie and do not fear the Lord of Death. Since you are a mental body you cannot die even if you are killed and cut up. You are really the natural form of emptiness, so there is no need to fear. The Lords of Death are the natural form of emptiness, your own confused projections, and you are emptiness, a mental body of unconscious tendencies. Emptiness cannot harm emptiness, the uncharacterized cannot harm the uncharacterized. External Lords of Death, gods, evil spirits, the Bull-headed demon and so on, have no reality apart from your own confused projections, so recognize this. At this moment recognize everything as the bardo. ⁑

"Meditate on the samādhi of the Great Symbol. If you do not know how to meditate, look closely at the nature of what makes you afraid, and you will see emptiness which has no nature whatever: this is called the dharmakāya. But this emptiness is not negation, its nature is frightening, mind with great awareness and clarity: this is the mind of the saṃbhogakāya. The emptiness and the luminosity are not two separate things, but the nature of emptiness is luminosity and the nature of luminosity is emptiness. Now the indivisible emptiness-luminosity, the naked mind, is stripped bare and dwells in its uncreated state: this is the svabhāvikakāya. Its own natural energy arises everywhere without obstruction: this is the compassionate nirmāṇakāya. ⸭

"O child of noble family, see in this way without distraction. As soon as you recognize, you will attain complete enlightenment in the four kāyas. Do not be distracted. This is the dividing-line where buddhas and sentient beings are separated. It is said of this moment: ⸭

In an instant, they are separated,
in an instant, complete enlightenment. ⁑

"Until yesterday you were distracted, so although so much of the bardo state has appeared you have not recognized, and you have so much fear. If you are distracted now, the rope of compassion will be cut off and you will go to a place where there is no liberation, so be careful." ⁑

By being shown like this, even though he did not recognize before, he will recognize here and attain liberation. If he is a layman who does not know how to meditate like this, one should say these words: ⁑

"O child of noble family, if you do not know how to meditate like this, remember the Buddha, the Dharma and the Saṅgha, and the Lord of Great Compassion, and supplicate them. Meditate on all the terrifying projections as the Lord of Great Compassion or as your yidam. Remember your guru and the secret transmission name you had in the human world, and tell it to the Dharma King, the Lord of Death. Even if you fall down the precipice you will not be hurt, so give up fear and terror." ⁝

By being shown in these words, even though he was not liberated before he will be liberated here. But because of the possibility that he may not recognize and so not be liberated, it is very important to make another effort, so one should call the dead person by name again and say these words: ⁝

"These present experiences will throw you into states of joy and sadness alternately at each moment, like a catapult, so now do not create any feeling of passion and aggression. ⁝

"If you are going to be born in a higher realm, at the time when experiences of the higher realms occur your relatives in the place you have left are sacrificing many animals dedicated for the sake of the dead, so impure thoughts will arise in you and you will feel violent anger, which will cause you to be born as a hell-being. So whatever is done in the place you have left, do not get angry but meditate on kindness.

"If you are attached to the possessions you have left behind, or if you feel attached to them through knowing that someone else is owning and enjoying your things, you will get angry with the people you have left behind, and that will certainly cause you to be born as a hell-being or a hungry ghost, even if you were going to reach a higher state. In any case, even if you are attached to the things you have left behind, you cannot get them; it is no use to you, so give up attachment and yearning for your possessions; abandon them, make a firm decision. Whoever is enjoying your things, do not be possessive but let them go. With one-pointed concentration think that you are offering them to your guru and the Three Jewels, and remain in a state of desirelessness.⸫

"When the kaṅkani ritual for the dead is recited for you and the 'purification from lower realms' and so on are performed for your sake, with the subtle supernatural perception resulting from your karma you will see them being done impurely, sleepily, inattentively and so on, with careless behavior without observance of the samaya vows, and you will be aware of lack of faith and feelings of disbelief, sinful actions through fear, and impurities in the rituals, and so you will think, 'Alas, they are deceiving me, surely they are deceiving me!' Thinking this you will have great sorrow and despair, and on top of not feeling pure devotion you will disbelieve and lose faith, and that will certainly cause you to go to the lower realms. It is

no use but very harmful, so however impurely the rituals are performed by the
spiritual friends you have left behind, think
with pure faith and devotion, 'Well! My
projections must be impure; how can there
be impurity in Buddha's words? These are
caused by my own impure projections, like
seeing the faults of my own face reflected
in a mirror. As for these people, their body
is the Saṅgha, their speech is the holy
Dharma, and their mind is the nature of
the Buddha, therefore I take refuge in
them.' Then whatever is done in the place
you have left will help you, so it is very
important to have pure thoughts in this
way; do not forget. ⁑

"If you are going to be born in one of
the three lower realms, at the time when
experiences of them occur your relatives
in the place you have left are performing
virtuous rituals free from sin, and gurus
and teachers are practicing holy dharma

with absolute purity of body, speech and mind, so you will feel great joy on seeing them, and that will immediately cause you to be born in a higher realm, even if you were going to fall down into the three lower realms, so it is very helpful. Therefore it is very important not to have impure thoughts but to feel pure devotion without prejudice, so be careful. ⁑

"O child of noble family, to sum up, now your mind in the bardo state has no support, so it is light and mobile, and whatever thought arises in it, good or bad, is very powerful; so do not think of any evil actions but remember the practice of virtue. If you have no practice, feel devotion and pure thoughts. Supplicate your yidam and the Lord of Great Compassion, and say this inspiration-prayer with intense concentration: ⁑

> When parted from beloved friends,
>   wandering alone,

my own projections' empty forms appear,
may the buddhas send out the power of
    their compassion
so that the bardo's terrors do not come.
When I suffer through the power of evil
    karma,
may my yidam clear away all suffering;
when the sound of dharmatā roars like a
    thousand thunders,
may it all become the sound of the six
    syllables.
When I follow my karma, without a
    refuge,
may the Lord of Great Compassion be my
    refuge;
when I suffer the karma of unconscious
    tendencies,
may the samādhi of bliss and luminosity
    arise. ⁞

Say this prayer fervently; it will certainly
lead you on the path. Be absolutely con-

vinced that it is not false, this is very important." ⸭

When this is said, he will remember and recognize and so attain liberation. But even though one does this many times, recognition is difficult because of the influence of much evil karma, so it is very helpful to repeat it again many times. Calling the dead person again by name one should say these words: ⸭

"O child of noble family, if you have not understood what has gone before, from now on the body you had in your past life will grow fainter and your future body will become clearer, so you will feel sad and think, 'I am suffering like this, so now I shall look for whatever kind of body appears,' and you will move about, backwards and forwards, towards anything that appears. The six lights of the six realms of existence will shine, and the one in which you are going to be born because of your karma will shine most brightly.⁑

"O child of noble family, listen. If you ask what the six lights are: the soft white light of the gods will shine, and similarly the red light of the jealous gods, the blue light of human beings, the green light of the animals, the yellow light of the hungry ghosts, and the smoke-colored light of hell-beings; these are the six lights. At that moment your body will also take on the color of the place where you are going to be born.⁑

"O child of noble family, at this time the essential point of the instruction is very important: whatever light shines, meditate on that as the Lord of Great Compassion. Meditate on the thought that when the light appears it is the Lord of Great Compassion. This is the most profound essential point, it is extremely important and prevents birth.⁑

"Meditate for a long time on whichever deity is your yidam, as a vision without any real nature of its own, like an illusion. This is called the pure illusory body. Then let the yidam disappear from the edges inwards, and rest for a while in the inconceivable state of emptiness-luminosity which consists in nothing whatever. Meditate again on the yidam, then again on the luminosity. Meditate like this alternately, and after that let your mind too disappear from the edges inwards. Wherever there is space there is mind, and wherever there is mind there is the dharmakāya; rest in the state of simplicity and selflessness of the dharmakāya." ⸙

In this state birth is prevented and he will become a buddha. But those whose practice was poor and who were not adept in meditation will not understand, and still confused will wander to the entrance of a womb, so the instructions for closing the womb-entrance are very important. One should call the dead person by name and say these words: ⁚

"O child of noble family, if you have not recognized what has gone before, now you will feel that you are moving upwards or across or downwards by the force of karma, so at this moment meditate on the Lord of Great Compassion; remember! ⁚

"Then you will have the experience, like that which was described before, of whirlwinds, snowstorms and hailstorms, darkness closing round and many men chasing you, and you will escape from them. Those without merit will feel that they are escaping to a place of suffering, but those with merit will feel that they are arriving in a place of joy. ⁚

"At this time, O child of noble family, all the signs of the country and place where you are going to be born will appear; so now listen without distraction, for there are many very profound essential points of instruction. Although you have not understood these secrets of recognition before, even one whose practice was very poor will get the point here, so listen.⁝

"At this time it is very important to take great care with the method of closing the entrance of the womb. There are two methods: stopping the person who is entering, and closing the womb-entrance which is being entered. This is the instruction for stopping the person who is entering:⁝

"O child of noble family, (name), clearly visualize whichever deity is your yidam, as a vision with no real nature of its own, like an illusion or the moon in water. If you have no specific yidam it is the Lord of Great Compassion himself; visualize him vividly. Then let the yidam disappear from the edges inwards, and meditate on the luminosity-emptiness without any object of thought. This is the profound secret; it is said that by means of it the womb is not entered, so meditate in this way. ፨

"But if this does not stop you and you are just about to enter a womb, there are profound instructions for closing the womb-entrance which is about to be entered, so listen. Repeat after me these words from "The Main Verses of the Bardo": ፨

Now when the bardo of becoming dawns
      upon me,
I will concentrate my mind one-pointedly
and strive to prolong the results of
      good karma,
close the womb-entrance and think
      of resistance;
this is the time when perseverance and
      pure thought are needed,

abandon jealousy, and meditate on
the guru with his consort. ⸪

Say these words clearly aloud and arouse your memory; it is very important to meditate on their meaning and put it into practice. ⸪

"This is the meaning: 'Now when the bardo of becoming dawns upon me' means that now you are wandering in the bardo of becoming. As signs of this, if you look into water you will not see your reflection, and your body has no shadow. Now there is no material body of flesh and blood, but these are signs of the mental body wandering in the bardo of becoming. So now you must concentrate your mind one-pointedly without distraction; just now that one-pointed concentration is the most important thing. It is like controlling a horse with a bridle. Whatever you concentrate on will come about, so do not think of evil actions, but remember the dharma, the teachings, the transmissions, and the authorizations for texts such as this "Liberation through Hearing" which you received in the human world, and strive to prolong the results of good karma. It is very important. Do not forget, do not be distracted. Now is the time which is the dividing-line between going up and going down; now is the time when by slipping into laziness even for a moment you will suffer for ever; now is the time when by concentrating one-pointedly you will be happy for ever. Concentrate your mind one-pointedly; strive to prolong the results of good karma. ❖

Now the time has come to close the womb-entrance. It is said:

> Close the womb entrance and think
>   of resistance;
> this is the time when perseverance and
>   pure thought are needed. ❖

Now that time has come. First the womb-entrance should be closed, and there are five methods of closing it, so understand them well. ॐ

"O child of noble family, at this time projections of men and women making love will appear. When you see them, do not enter in between them, but remember, and meditate on the man and woman as the guru and his consort. Mentally prostrate yourself and make offerings with deep devotion, and ask for teachings; as soon as you concentrate intensely on this thought the womb-entrance will certainly be closed. ॐ

"But if this does not close it and you are just about to enter a womb, meditate on the guru and his consort as your own yidam, or the Lord of Great Compassion, with his consort, and mentally make offerings to them. With intense devotion ask them to bestow spiritual attainments; this will close the womb-entrance. ⁑

"But if this does not close it and you are just about to enter a womb, here is the third instruction on turning away passion and aggression. There are four kinds of birth: birth from an egg, birth from a womb, spontaneous birth and birth from moisture. Of these, birth from an egg and birth from a womb are similar. As above, there will be projections of males and females in sexual union, and if you enter a womb at this moment through the power of passion and aggression, you will be born as a horse, bird, dog, human being and so on, whatever it may be. If you are going to be born as a male, you will experience yourself as male, and feel violent aggression toward the father and jealousy and desire for the mother. If you are going to be born as a female you will experience yourself as female, and feel intense envy and jealousy of the mother and intense desire and passion for the father. This will cause you to enter the path leading to the womb, and you will experience self-existing bliss in the midst of the meeting of the sperm and ovum. From that blissful state you will lose consciousness, and the embryo will grow round and oblong and so on until the body matures and comes out from the mother's womb. You will open your eyes, and you have turned into a puppy; from first being a man you have now become a dog, so you will suffer in a dog-kennel, or similarly in a pigsty or an ant-hill or a worm-hole, or else you may be born as a young bull or goat or lamb and so on. There is no returning here; you will endure all kinds of suffering from a state of great stupidity and ignorance. Circling like this around the six realms of existence, of hell-beings, hungry ghosts and so on, you will be tormented by boundless

suffering. There is nothing more powerful
or terrifying than this; alas! alas! Those
who do not have a guru's sacred teachings
will fall down the great precipice of samsāra in this manner, and endure endless,
unbearable suffering; so therefore listen to
my words, and understand this instruction
of mine. ⁑

"Now the instruction for closing the
womb-entrance by turning away passion
and aggression is given; listen and understand. It is said: ⁑

> *Close the womb-entrance and think*
>   *of resistance;*
> *this is the time when perseverance*
>   *and pure thought are needed,*
> *abandon jealousy, and meditate on*
>   *the guru with his consort.* ⁑

As above, you will have feelings of jealousy;
if you are going to be born as a male you
will love the mother and hate the father,

and if you are going to be born as a female you will love the father and hate the mother. So at this time there is a profound instruction. ⁑

"O child of noble family, when passion and aggression arise like this, meditate in this way: 'Alas! I am a being with such evil karma that I have been wandering like this in saṃsāra until now, through clinging to passion and aggression. If I go on feeling passion and aggression like this, I shall wander in saṃsāra endlessly, and sink into the depths of the ocean of suffering for a long time; so now I will feel no passion or aggression at all. Alas! Now I will never again feel passion and aggression.' By concentrating your mind intensely and one-pointedly on this thought, that itself will close the womb-entrance, so the tantras say. O child of noble family, do not be distracted; concentrate your mind one-pointedly. ⁑

"But if, even after doing this, the womb-entrance is not closed and you are about to enter a womb, then it should be closed by the instruction on the unreal and illusory nature of everything. Meditate in this way: 'Alas! The father and mother, the great storm, the whirlwind, the thunder, the terrifying projections and all these apparent phenomena are illusory in their real nature. However they appear, they are not real. All substances are false and untrue. They are like a mirage, they are not permanent, they are not changeless. What is the use of desire? What is the use of fear? It is regarding the non-existent as existent. All these are projections of my mind, and since the mind itself is illusory and non-existent from the beginning, from where externally do they arise like this? I did not understand in this way before, and so I believed the nonexistent to exist, the untrue to be true, the illusion to be real; therefore

I have wandered in saṃsāra for so long. And if I do not realize that they are illusions, I shall still wander in saṃsāra for a long time and certainly fall into the muddy swamp of suffering. Now they are all like dreams, like illusions, like echoes, like cities of the gandharvas, like mirages, like images, like optical illusions, like the moon in water; they are not real, even for a moment. Certainly they are not true, but false!' ⸭

"By concentrating one-pointedly on this conviction, belief in their reality is destroyed, and when one is inwardly convinced in such a way, belief in a self is counteracted. If you understand unreality like this from the bottom of your heart, the womb-entrance will certainly be closed. ⸭

"But if, even after doing this, the belief in reality is not destroyed, and the womb-entrance is not closed, and you are about to enter a womb, there is a profound instruction.

"O child of noble family, if even after doing this the womb-entrance is not closed, now it should be closed by the fifth method, meditation on the luminosity, which should be done in this way: 'All substances are my own mind, and this mind is emptiness, unarisen and unobstructed.' Thinking this, keep your mind natural and undiluted, self-contained in its own nature like water poured into water, just as it is, loose, open and relaxed. By letting it rest naturally and loosely you can be sure that the womb-entrance to all four kinds of birth will certainly be closed."

Many true and profound instructions for closing the womb-entrance have been given above; it is impossible for anyone of high, average or low capacities, whichever he may be, not to be liberated by them. Why is this? Firstly because consciousness in the bardo state possesses supernatural perception of worldly things, so he can hear what I say; secondly, even if he was deaf and blind, now he has all the senses complete, so he can hear what is said; thirdly, being continually overcome by fear he is thinking undistractedly what to do, so he listens to what I say; and fourthly, as the consciousness has no support it comes directly to wherever the concentration is directed, so it is easy to guide. The mind is nine times more clear, so even if he is stupid, by force of karma the mind becomes so clear at this time that it can meditate on whatever is taught; essential points such as these are the reason. For the same reason it is also helpful to perform the rituals for the dead. ❖

Therefore it is very important to persevere in reading this "Great Liberation through Hearing" for up to nine days. Even if he is not liberated at one showing he will attain liberation at another. That is the reason why not one but many showings are necessary. ⁑

Even then, there are many kinds of people who were not used to doing good actions but were extremely skilled in doing evil actions right from the start, and through the influence of many powerful veils of error are not liberated, in spite of being shown and given these objects of meditation so many times above; so now, if the womb-entrance has not been closed before, a profound instruction for choosing the womb-entrance will be taught below. One should call on the buddhas and bodhisattvas for help and repeat the refuge,[19] then call the dead person by name three times and say these words: ⁑

"O child of noble family, (name,) who is dead, listen. Although you have been shown with the instructions above so many times, you have not understood, so now, if the womb-entrance has not been closed, the time has come to take a body. There are not one but many true and profound instructions for you to choose a womb-entrance, so understand and do not be distracted. Listen well with intense concentration and understand. ☙

"O child of noble family, now the signs and characteristics of the continent where you are going to be born will appear, so recognize them. Examine where you are going to be born and choose the continent. ☙

"If you are going to be born in the eastern continent, Noble Body, you will see a lake adorned with geese and ganders. Think of resistance and do not go there. Although it is full of happiness it is a place where dharma does not flourish, so do not enter it. ☙

"If you are going to be born in the southern continent, Rose-Apple Island, you will see luxurious, beautiful dwellings. You should enter it if you can.❖

"If you are going to be born in the western continent, Enjoyment of Wish-fulfilling Cows, you will see a lake adorned with horses and mares. Do not go there but come back here. Although it has great pleasures it is a place where dharma does not flourish, so do not enter it.❖

"If you are going to be born in the northern continent, Unpleasant Sound, you will see a lake adorned with cattle or with trees. Recognize them as signs of taking birth, and do not go there. Although it has long life and merits, dharma does not flourish there, so do not enter.❖

"If you are going to be born as a god, you will see beautiful many-storied temples made of various jewels. If you are fit to enter there you should enter.❖

"If you are going to be born as a jealous god, you will see beautiful groves, or what seem to be revolving wheels of fire. Do not enter there at all, but think of resistance. ⸪

"If you are going to be born as an animal, you will see as if through a mist rock-caves and holes in the ground and straw huts. Do not enter there. ⸪

"If you are going to be born as a hungry ghost, you will see tree-stumps and black shapes sticking up, shallow caves and black patches. If you go there you will be born as a hungry ghost and experience all kinds of suffering through hunger and thirst, so do not go there at all, but think of resistance and persevere strongly. ⸪

"If you are going to be born as a hell-being, you will hear songs sung by those of evil karma, or you will have to enter helplessly, or you will feel that you have gone into a dark land, with black and red houses, black pits and black roads. If you go there you will enter hell and experience unbearable suffering through heat and cold from which you will never get out. So do not go into its midst, do not enter at all, but be careful. It is said: 'Close the womb-entrance and think of resistance'; this is needed now. ⁑

"O child of noble family, even though you wish not to go, you have no power of your own, you are helplessly compelled to go. From behind the avengers of karma pursue you, and in front avengers and murderers drag you along; darkness, hurricanes, violent storms, noises, snow and rain, fierce hailstorms and snowstorms will whirl around you, and you will escape from them. Then in escaping you will look for a refuge, and you will find safety in the luxurious houses described before or in rock-shelters or holes in the ground, between trees, or in the round cavities of lotus flowers and so on. Hidden there, you will be afraid to come out, and you will think, 'I cannot go out of here now,' and through fear of leaving you will become very attached to that place. You are afraid of meeting those terrors of the bardo if you go outside, you feel extreme fear of them; and so you hide inside and take a body, however bad it may be, and will experience all kinds of suffering. That is a sign that demons and evil forces are obstructing you now, and at this time there is a profound instruction, so listen and understand. ⁑

"At this time of terror when you are helplessly pursued by the avengers, you should immediately visualize with your whole mind the Blessed Supreme Heruka or Hayagrīva or Vajrapāṇi, or your yidam if you have one, with a huge body and thick limbs, standing in a terrifying attitude of wrath which crushes all evil forces into dust. Separated from the avengers by his blessing and compassion, you will have the power to choose the entrance of a womb.

This is the true profound secret of the instruction, so understand it. ⁘

"O child of noble family, the gods of meditation and so on are born through the power of samādhi. A large class of evil spirits such as hungry ghosts and so on have changed their attitude while in the bardo state, then they are able to appear in various illusory forms of hungry ghosts and demons, and are transformed into that mental body itself. The hungry ghosts who dwell in the depths of the sea and the hungry ghosts who fly through space, and all the eighty thousand classes of negative forces and so on, have taken on that mental body by changing their attitude. At this time the best thing is to contemplate the Great Symbol of emptiness, but if you cannot do that, then take part in the play of illusion. If you cannot do that either, at least do not be attached to anything, but meditate on the yidam, the Lord of Great

Compassion, and you will become a sambhogakāya buddha in the bardo state.⁙

"O child of noble family, if you have to enter a womb in this way through force of karma, the instruction for choosing the entrance to a womb will now be taught. Listen! Do not go into whatever womb-entrance appears. If the avengers come and you cannot avoid entering, meditate on Hayagrīva. Since you now possess subtle supernatural perception you will know all the places in turn, so make a choice. There are two instructions; for transference to a pure buddha-realm and for choosing an impure saṃsāric womb-entrance, so act in this way:⁙

"Transference to the Pure Realm of Space, of purified faculties, is directed like this: 'Ah, how sad it is that I still remain in this muddy swamp of saṃsāra even now, after such a long time of countless ages without beginning or end, and while so many others have already become buddhas I have not been liberated. From this moment on I feel sickened at this saṃsāra, I dread it, I am worn out with it. Now it is time to get ready to escape, so I must bring about a spontaneous birth in a lotus flower at the feet of the buddha Amitābha in the western Blissful Realm.' With this thought concentrate intensely on the Blissful Realm in the west, it is vital to make this effort. Or else, if you direct intense concentration, one-pointedly and without distraction, toward whichever realm you wish, the Pure Realm, or Complete Joy, or the Densely Filled, or the Realm of Willow Leaves, or the Palm-tree Mountain, or the Palace of Lotus Light in Urgyan, you will immediately be born in that realm. Or if you wish to go into the presence of Lord Maitreya in the Joyful Realm, concentrate on this thought: 'At this moment in the bardo state the time has come for me to go into the presence of the Dharma King Maitreya in the Joyful Realm, so I will go,' and you will be born spontaneously in the heart of a lotus in the presence of Maitreya. ⸙

"Otherwise, if you cannot do this and wish to enter a womb, or find you have to enter one, there is an instruction for choosing an impure saṃsāric womb-entrance, so listen. As before, look at the continent you are going to choose with supernatural perception, and enter a place where dharma flourishes. ⸙

"If you are going to be spontaneously born in a filthy dung-heap, you will perceive that fetid mass as sweet-smelling, and you will feel attracted to it and be born there; so whatever appears, do not trust it, but put an end to the signs of desire and hatred, and choose a womb-entrance. ⸙

"Again, it is very important to concentrate like this: 'I will be born as a universal

emperor for the good of all sentient beings, or as a brāhmaṇa like a great sāla
tree, or as the son of a siddha, or in a
family of a pure lineage of dharma, or in a
family where the father and mother have
faith; and taking a body with merits which
can benefit all sentient beings, I will do
good.' Concentrating on this thought, the
womb should be entered. At this time you
should bless the womb you are entering as
a palace of the gods, and supplicate the
buddhas and bodhisattvas of the ten directions and the yidams, especially the Lord
of Great Compassion, and enter the womb
with the longing of a request for transmission. ⸭

"It is possible to make a mistake in
choosing the entrance of a womb like this,
by seeing a good womb-entrance as bad or
a bad one as good, under the influence of
karma, so now again the essential point of
the instruction is very important, so do

this: even if a womb-entrance appears good do not trust it, and even if it appears bad do not feel dislike of it. The true, profound, essential secret is to enter into the supreme state of equilibrium in which there is no good or bad, acceptance or rejection, passion or aggression."⁝

But, except for the few who are experienced in this, it is hard to get rid of the disease of bad unconscious tendencies, so to prevent him taking refuge among sinners of the poorest capacities, the lowest of the low, like beasts, if he cannot cut off passion and aggression in this way, one should call the dead person again by name and say these words:⁝

"O child of noble family, if you do not know how to choose a womb-entrance and cannot get rid of passion and aggression, whatever of the above experiences may arise, call on the name of the Three Jewels and take refuge in them. Supplicate the

Lord of Great Compassion. Go on with your head held high. Give up attachment and yearning for the relatives and friends, sons and daughters, you have left behind; they cannot help you. Enter now into the blue light of human beings or the white light of the gods; enter the jewelled palaces and the pleasure-gardens." ⸪

This should be repeated up to seven times. Then one should supplicate the buddhas and bodhisattvas, and read "The Bardo Prayer which Protects from Fear," "The Main Verses of the Bardo," and "Deliverance from the Dangerous Pathway of the Bardo" up to seven times. Then one should read "The Liberation through Wearing which Spontaneously Liberates the Skandhas," and "The Daily Practice which Spontaneously Liberates the Unconscious Tendencies," clearly and distinctly. ⸪

Thus, by acting rightly, yogins of high-

THE TIBETAN BOOK OF THE DEAD

est insight effect the ejection of consciousness in the bardo of the moment before death, and do not have to wander in the bardo state but bypass it and attain liberation. Below them, a few experienced people recognize the luminosity of the dharmatā after the bardo of the moment before death, and bypass and become buddhas. Those below them are liberated in accordance with their karmic results at one time or another when the peaceful and wrathful projections appear in the bardo of dharmatā during the following weeks. As there are many stages they will recognize whichever is appropriate and attain liberation. ‡

But those whose good karmic results are weak and who have many veils of error and very bad karma must wander on down to the bardo of becoming; but as there are many showings, like the steps of a ladder, they will recognize at one or another and

be liberated. But if those whose good karmic results are very weak do not recognize
during the above and are overpowered by
fear, there is a series of instructions in turn
for closing the womb-entrance and for
choosing a womb-entrance, so they will
recognize at one or another, and trusting
the object of meditation attain the highest
state of boundless virtue. ⸭

Even the lowest of the low, like beasts,
are turned back from the lower realms by
the virtue of taking refuge; they will attain
a precious human body complete with all
the freedoms and good opportunities, and
in their next life meet a holy guru, a spiritual friend, so they will get instruction
and be liberated. ⸭

If this teaching is received during the
bardo of becoming, the instruction pro-
longs one's good karmic results, like putting a pipe into a broken water-channel. It
is impossible even for all great sinners not

to be liberated when they hear this teaching. Why is this? Because during the bardo both the compassionate invitation of all the peaceful and wrathful buddhas and deities and the invitation of the tempters and negative forces come together, so just by hearing the teaching at this time their attitude is influenced and they attain liberation. Influence is easy because the mental body has no basis of flesh and blood. However far they have wandered in the bardo state, they see and hear with subtle karmic supernatural perception and they come; this is extremely helpful, for then they understand and their mind is instantaneously influenced. It is like the device of a catapult, or like a huge tree-trunk which cannot be moved by a hundred men, but when it is put in water can be taken wherever one wants in a moment; it is like controlling a horse with a bridle. ⁝

Therefore one should approach all who

have died, and if the corpse is present a friend should read this reminder again and again until blood and pus come out of the nostrils. Meanwhile the corpse should remain undisturbed. The observances for this are: animals should not be sacrificed for dedication to the dead person; in the presence of the corpse friends and relations should not weep and mourn and make a noise, which may be done elsewhere; and as many acts of virtue as possible should be done. ⁝

As well as this teaching of "The Great Liberation through Hearing" it is very good if any of the other teachings joined to the end of this instruction are also read. One should read this continually and learn the word-meanings and terms by heart; then when death is certain and the signs of death have been recognized, if one's condition allows one should read it aloud oneself and contemplate it, and if one is not able to do that it should be given to a dharma-brother or dharma-sister to read, for this reminder will certainly liberate, there is no doubt. This teaching does not need any practice, it is a profound instruction which liberates just by being seen and heard and read. This profound instruction leads great sinners on the secret path. If one does not forget its words and terms even when being chased by seven dogs, the instruction liberates in the bardo of the moment before death. Even if the buddhas of the past, present and future were to search, they would not find a better teaching than this. ⁑

iti ⁑

The bardo instruction
which liberates human beings,
the profound innermost essence,
"The Great Liberation through Hearing."

This treasure was discovered
by the siddha Karma-Lingpa in
the mountain of Gampo-dar.
May it benefit the dharma
and all sentient beings. ⁑

sarvamaṅgalam ⁑

INSPIRATION-PRAYERS

These "inspiration-prayers" are taken from the collection of terma texts connected with Bardo Thötröl. They are all mentioned as devotional exercises in the Bardo Thötröl itself, and several verses from them are quoted as part of the instructions to the dead person. The word which is often translated simply as prayer means literally "wish-path" (Tibetan smon-lam). It is not a request to an external diety, but a method of purifying and directing the mind. It acts as inspiration by arousing the mind's inherent desire for good, which attracts the fulfilment of its aim.

INSPIRATION-PRAYER
CALLING ON THE
BUDDHAS AND
BODHISATTVAS
FOR RESCUE

At the time of one's death, one should always call on the Buddhas and Bodhisattvas for rescue. One should make material and mental offerings to the Three Jewels, and holding fragrant incense in one's hand, say these words with intense power of concentration:

O Buddhas and Bodhisattvas dwelling in the ten directions, compassionate, all-knowing, with the five kinds of eyes, loving, protectors of all sentient beings, come to this place by the power of compassion

and accept these material and mental offerings. ⸖

O Compassionate Ones, you possess
understanding wisdom, loving compassion,
effective action, and protecting power beyond the reach of thought. O Compassionate Ones, this person, (name), is going
from this world to the other shore, he is
leaving this world, he is dying without
choice, he has no friends, he is suffering
greatly, he has no refuge, he has no protector, he has no allies, the light of this life
has set, he is going to another world, he is
entering dense darkness, he is falling down
a deep precipice, he is entering a thick for-
est, he is pursued by the power of karma,
he is entering a great wilderness, he is
swept away by a great ocean, he is driven
on by the wind of karma, he is going
where there is no solid ground, he is em-
barking on a great battle, he is seized by
the great evil spirit, he is terrified by the

messengers of the Lord of Death, he is entering existence after existence because of his karma, he is helpless, the time has come when he must go on alone without a friend. ⁝

O Compassionate Ones, be a refuge to him, (name), who has no refuge, protect him, defend him, keep him from the great darkness of the bardo, turn him aside from the great hurricane of karma, protect him from the great fear of the Lord of Death, deliver him from the long and dangerous pathway of the bardo. O Compassionate Ones, do not let your compassion be small, rescue him, do not let him go to the three lower realms, do not forget your former vows but quickly send out the power of your compassion. ⁝

O Buddhas and Bodhisattvas, do not let your compassion and skillful means for him, (name), be small, seize him with compassion, do not let a sentient being fall into the power of evil karma. ⁝

May the Three Jewels be a refuge from suffering in the bardo. ⁝

This should be said three times with deep devotion by oneself and all others. Then "The Liberation through Hearing," "Deliverance from the Dangerous Pathway of the Bardo," and "The Bardo Prayer which Protects from Fear" should be read. ⁝

THE MAIN VERSES
OF THE SIX BARDOS

*Now when the bardo of birth is dawning
    upon me,*
*I will abandon laziness for which life has no
    time,*
*enter the undistracted path of study, reflection
    and meditation,*
*making projections and mind the path, and
    realize the three kāyas;*
now that I have once attained a human body,
*there is no time on the path for the mind to
    wander.* ∻

*Now when the bardo of dreams is dawning
    upon me,*
*I will abandon the corpse-like sleep of careless
    ignorance,*
*and let my thoughts enter their natural state
    without distraction;*

controlling and transforming dreams in
    luminosity,
I will not sleep like any animal
but unify completely sleep and practice. ⁞

Now when the bardo of samādhi-meditation
    dawns upon me,
I will abandon the crowd of distractions and
    confusions,
and rest in the boundless state without
    grasping or disturbance;
firm in the two practices: visualization and
    complete,
at this time of meditation, one-pointed, free
    from activity,
I will not fall into the power of confused
    emotions. ⁞

Now when the bardo of the moment before
    death dawns upon me,
I will abandon all grasping, yearning and
    attachment,
enter undistracted into clear awareness of
    the teaching,

and eject my consciousness into the space of
    unborn mind;
as I leave this compound body of flesh and
    blood
I will know it to be a transitory illusion. ❖

Now when the bardo of dharmatā dawns
    upon me,
I will abandon all thoughts of fear and terror,
I will recognize whatever appears as my pro-
    jection
and know it to be a vision of the bardo;
now that I have reached this crucial point,
I will not fear the peaceful and wrathful ones,
    my own projections. ❖

Now when the bardo of becoming dawns upon
    me,
I will concentrate my mind one-pointedly,
and strive to prolong the results of good
    karma,
close the womb-entrance and think of
    resistance;

this is the time when perseverance and pure
   thought are needed,
abandon jealousy, and meditate on the guru
   with his consort. ⁝

With mind far off, not thinking of death's
   coming,
performing these meaningless activities,
returning empty-handed now would be complete confusion;
the need is recognition, holy dharma,
so why not practise dharma at this very
   moment?
From the mouths of siddhas come these words:
If you do not keep your guru's teaching in
   your heart
will you not become your own deceiver? ⁝

INSPIRATION-PRAYER FOR DELIVERANCE FROM THE DANGEROUS PATHWAY OF THE BARDO

Homage to the gurus, yidams and ḍākinīs,
with their great love may they lead us on
the path. ⁝

When through confusion I wander in saṃsāra,
on the undistracted light-path of study,
reflection and meditation,
may the gurus of the sacred lineage go before
me,
their consorts the hosts of ḍākinīs behind me;
help me to cross the bardo's dangerous
pathway
and bring me to the perfect buddha state. ⁝

*When through intense ignorance I wander
   in saṃsāra,*

*on the luminous light-path of the dharma-
   dhātu wisdom,*

may Blessed Vairocana go before me,

*his consort the Queen of Vajra Space
   behind me;*

*help me to cross the bardo's dangerous
   pathway*

and bring me to the perfect buddha state. ⁑

*When through intense aggression I wander
   in saṃsāra,*

*on the luminous light-path of the mirror-like
   wisdom,*

may Blessed Vajrasattva go before me,

his consort Buddha-Locanā behind me;

*help me to cross the bardos dangerous
   pathway*

and bring me to the perfect buddha state. ⁑

*When through intense pride I wander in
   saṃsāra,*

on the luminous light-path of the wisdom of
  equality,
may Blessed Ratnasaṃbhava go before me,
his consort Māmakī behind me;
help me to cross the bardo's dangerous
  pathway
and bring me to the perfect buddha state. ⁝

When through intense desire I wander in
  saṃsāra,
on the luminous light-path of discriminating
  wisdom,
may Blessed Amitābha go before me,
his consort Pāṇḍaravāsinī behind me;
help me to cross the bardo's dangerous
  pathway
and bring me to the perfect buddha state. ⁝

When through intense envy I wander in
  saṃsāra,
on the luminous light-path of action-
  accomplishing wisdom,
may Blessed Amoghasiddhi go before me,
his consort Samaya-Tārā behind me;

*help me to cross the bardo's dangerous
    pathway*
and bring me to the perfect buddha state. ⁝

*When through strong unconscious tendencies
    I wander in saṃsāra,*
*on the luminous light-path of the innate
    wisdom,*
may the vidyādhara warriors go before me,
their consorts the host of ḍākinīs behind me;
*help me to cross the bardo's dangerous
    pathway*
and bring me to the perfect buddha state. ⁝

*When through fierce confused projections
    I wander in saṃsāra,*
on the light-path of abandoning all fear,
*may the Blessed Ones, peaceful and wrathful,
    go before me,*
*the host of ḍākinīs, Queens of Space,
    behind me;*
*help me to cross the bardo's dangerous
    pathway*
and bring me to the perfect buddha state. ⁝

May the element of space not rise up as
    an enemy,
may I see the Realm of the blue buddha.
May the element of water not rise up as
    enemy,
may I see the realm of the white buddha.
May the element of earth not rise up as
    an enemy,
may I see the realm of the yellow buddha.
May the element of fire not rise up as an
    enemy,
may I see the realm of the red buddha.
May the element of air not rise up as an
    enemy.
may I see the realm of the green buddha.
May the rainbow of the elements not rise up
    as enemies,
may I see the realms of all the buddhas.
May the sounds, lights and rays not rise up
    as enemies,
may I see the infinite realms of the Peaceful
    and Wrathful Ones.
May I know all the sounds as my own sound,

may I know all the lights as my own light,
may I know all the rays as my own ray.
May I spontaneously know the bardo as
    myself,
may I attain the realms of the three kāyas. ⁘

THE BARDO PRAYER
WHICH PROTECTS
FROM FEAR

When the journey of my life has reached
   its end,
and since no relatives go with me from this
   world
I wander in the bardo state alone,
may the peaceful and wrathful buddhas send
   out the power of their compassion
and clear away the dense darkness of ignorance. ⚇

When parted from beloved friends, wandering
   alone,
my own projections' empty forms appear,
may the buddhas send out the power of their
   compassion
so that the bardo's terrors do not come. ⚇

When the five luminous lights of wisdom
    shine,
fearlessly may I recognize myself;
when the forms of the peaceful and wrathful
    ones appear,
fearless and confident may I recognize the
    bardo. ⁑

When I suffer through the power of evil
    karma,
may the peaceful and wrathful buddhas clear
    away suffering;
when the sound of dharmatā roars like a
    thousand thunders,
may it be transformed into the sound of
    mahāyāna teaching. ⁑

When I follow my karma, without a refuge,
may the peaceful and wrathful buddhas be
    my refuge;
when I suffer the karma of unconscious
    tendencies,
may the samādhi of bliss and luminosity
    arise. ⁑

At the moment of spontaneous birth in the
  bardo of becoming,
may the false teachings of the tempters not
  arise;
when I arrive wherever I wish by supernatural
  power,
may the illusory terrors of evil karma not
  arise. ⁘

When savage beasts of prey are roaring,
may it become the sound of dharma, the six
  syllables;
when I am chased by snow, rain, wind and
  darkness,
may I receive the clear, divine eye of wisdom. ⁘

May all sentient beings of the same realm in
  the bardo,
free from jealousy, be born in a higher state;
when great thirst and hunger are caused by
  passions,
may the pain of thirst and hunger, heat and
  cold, not arise. ⁘

When I see my future parents in union,
may I see the peaceful and wrathful buddhas
    with their consorts;
with power to choose my birthplace, for the
    good of others,
may I receive a perfect body adorned with
    auspicious signs. ⁑

Obtaining for myself a perfect human body,
may all who see and hear me at once be
    liberated;
may I not follow all my evil karma,
but follow and increase what merit I may
    have. ⁑

Wherever I am born, at that very place,
may I meet the yidam of this life face to face;
knowing how to walk and talk as soon as I
    am born,
may I attain the power of non-forgetfulness
    and remembrance of past lives. ⁑

In all the stages of learning, high, middle
    and low,

may I understand just by hearing, thinking
    and seeing;
wherever I am born, may that land be blessed,
so that all sentient beings may be happy. ፧

O peaceful and wrathful buddhas, may I and
    others
become like you yourselves, just as you are,
with your forms and your auspicious marks,
your retinues, your long life and your
    realms. ፧

Samantabhadra, the peaceful and wrathful
    ones, infinite compassion,
the power of truth of the pure dharmatā,
and followers of tantra in one-pointed
    meditation:
may their blessings fulfill this inspiration-
    prayer. ፧

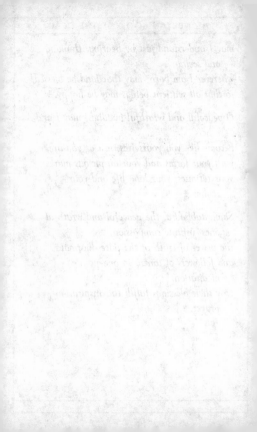

NOTES

1. This mark distinguishes all terma texts (see Foreword) and is a symbol to seal and protect them. It is found throughout the texts in place of the usual Tibetan punctuation mark — a short vertical line. Since English punctuation is more complicated, terma marks are placed in the translation only at the end of paragraphs and lines of verse.

2. Ejection of consciousness (Tib. 'pho-ba) is part of the Pure Land practice and one of the Six Yogas of Nāropā. By means of it the yogin learns how to shoot his consciousness up through the crown of his head into a visualized image, and at death he is able to direct it to the dharma-kāya realm. Details of this practice can be found in Herbert Guenther's *The Life and Teaching of Nāropā* (Oxford) and in Garma C. C. Chang's *Esoteric Teachings of the Tibetan Tantra* (Aurora Press).

3. Dharma-brothers and dharma-sisters are disciples of the same guru.

4. The Three Jewels are the Buddha, or principle of enlightenment; the Dharma, or teaching

which proclaims enlightenment; and the Saṅgha, or community which practices the Dharma.

5. The position of Gautama Buddha at his death: lying stretched out on the right side, with the right hand under the head.

6. The Great Symbol (Tib. phyag-rgya-chen-po, Skt. mahāmudrā) is a tantric meditation practice in which the whole of experience is transformed into the deity and the maṇḍala; in this state the great bliss (mahāsukha) is produced from the union of the male and female aspects of practice—skillful means or compassion, and knowledge or emptiness (upāya and prajñā). It is direct perception of the sacredness and vividness of life.

7. Samantabhadra and Samantabhadrī (Tib. kun-tu-bzang-po and kun-tu-bzang-mo) symbolize the inseparability of compassion and knowledge, the two coefficients of enlightenment. As the embodiment of the dharmakāya they are the origin of the five buddha families, who emanate from them and appear on the saṃbhoga-kāya level. In this sense, in the Nyingma tradition, Samantabhadra is known as the ādibuddha, or primordial buddha. It is also the

name of a bodhisattva, who appears on the third day of the bardo.

8. These practices are two complementary styles of meditation in tantric yoga. In the generation stage (Tib. bskyed-rim, Skt. utpattikrama) the yogin visualizes the deities and identifies himself with them; in the perfection stage (Tib. rdzogs-rim, Skt. saṃpannakrama) everything is dissolved into emptiness and formlessness.

9. The yidam is a particular deity which represents the disciple's innate enlightened nature, chosen by his guru to correspond to his own characteristics and the practice he is following. It is said that Avalokiteśvara, the Lord of Great Compassion, is suitable for everyone, so "an ordinary person," one who has not been given a specific yidam, should meditate on him.

10. Illustrations and descriptions of these eight female bodhisattvas can be found in many sources, such as the pantheons published by Lokesh Chandra, W. E. Clark's *Two Lamaistic Pantheons* or B. Bhattacharyya's *The Indian Buddhist Iconography,* in which they appear as "dance deities" and "goddesses of direction." Waddell calls them mātṛs or mother-goddesses, in connection with the maṇḍala offering, but they are not the same as the Hindu mātṛs, as Evans-

Wentz suggests. They are essentially goddesses of worship, who offer the objects of sensual pleasure to the principle of enlightenment.

11. The ten stages in the development of a bodhisattva.

12. Three terms are mentioned in the Tibetan: gdung, ring-bsrel and sku-gzugs, or in Sanskrit: śarīram. These are all similar remains left behind when the corpse of an accomplished yogin or siddha has been burned. They are like shining round stones, white or greenish in color, and are kept as relics and often eaten just before death.

13. For Great Symbol see note 6. The Great Completion (Tib. rdzogs-pa-chenpo, Skt. mahāsampanna) is a stage of meditation equivalent to atiyoga or mahā-ati. It penetrates beyond even the apparently ultimate vision of the Great Symbol into a further experience of openness and formlessness. This practice was taught by Vimalamitra, a contemporary of Padmasambhava, and developed in the Nyingma tradition. The two practices, Great Symbol and Great Completion, were unified by Rangjung-Dorje, the third Karmapa.

14. The "Liberation through Wearing" (Tib. btags-grol) is another of the six bardo instructions of

Padmasaṃbhava. It is a short text consisting mostly of mantras, which is tied to the corpse as an amulet.

15. The Glorious Great Buddha-Heruka is a combination of the Buddha-Heruka and the Great Heruka, who is the origin of the herukas of the five families, as described in the Commentary. In paintings (thankas) of the wrathful deities, the Great Heruka appears in the center, the counterpart of Samantabhadra in the maṇḍala of the peaceful deities, while the Buddha-Heruka is placed below him.

16. The gaurīs, meaning "white," are a group of eight goddesses collectively named after the first of them, who is the only white one. In the Tibetan texts of the *Bardo Thötröl*, their names are kept in Sanskrit, but most are in a corrupted form with slight differences in each blockprint (Evans-Wentz calls them the Keurima, for instance). They appear in many other tantric texts, but two names here, Pramohā and Śmaśānī, are different from the usual list. Pramohā or Pramo, meaning "deluder" probably corresponds to Ḍombī, the low-caste woman who is a symbol of passion in tantric poetry; while Śmaśānī, "she who dwells in the charnel-ground," seems to be the most reasonable San-

skrit name which can be deduced from the Tibetan form, Smeśani, and would correspond to
Śavarī, the "ascetic" or "mountain-dweller." It
is not possible to identify these goddesses
purely by their descriptions, as they appear differently in the various sources. The piśācīs (Tib.
phra-men-ma) are flesh-eating goddesses with
bird and animal heads. Their name means
"striped" or "variegated," referring to the different colors of their heads and bodies. The
yoginīs are also called "powerful lady" (Tib.
dbang-phyug-ma, Skt. īśvarī). Most of them
were originally Hindu goddesses, absorbed into
Buddhism. In the text their names are all translated into Tibetan, but Sanskrit versions are
given here as well as the translations since many
are well known.

17. The six-syllabled mantra of Avalokiteśvara, *oṃ
maṇipadme hūṃ.*

18. The vajra seat is the seat on which Gautama
Buddha sat when he attained enlightenment at
Bodhgayā.

19. The refuge formula of commitment to the Buddhist path: I take refuge in the Buddha, I take
refuge in the Dharma, I take refuge in the
Saṅgha.

LIBRARY OF CONGRESS

CATALOGING-IN-PUBLICATION DATA

Karma-gliṅ-pa, 14th cent. [Bar do thos grol. English]
The Tibetan book of the dead: the great liberation
through hearing in the Bardo/by Guru Rinpoche
according to Karma Lingpa; translated by
Francesca Fremantle & Chögyam Trungpa.
    p.   cm. — (Shambhala pocket classics)
    Translation of: Bar do thos grol.
    ISBN 0-87773-675-8 (pbk.: acid-free paper)
    1. Intermediate state — Buddhism — Early works to
1800.   2. Death — Religious aspects — Buddhism — Early
    works to 1800.   3. Funeral rites and cere-
monies. Buddhist — Early works to 1800 — China
        — Tibet.   I. Fremantle, Francesca.
        II. Trungpa, Chögyam, 1939–
            III. Title.   IV. Series.
    BQ4490.K3713   1992   91-50798
    294.3´423 — dc20   CIP

THE TIBETAN BOOK OF THE DEAD
is also available as an audio tape
from Shambhala Lion Editions.

WALDEN by Henry David Thoreau

THE WAY OF A PILGRIM
Translated by Olga Savin

THE WAY OF CHUANG TZU
by Thomas Merton